Self-Directed

GROWTH

Douglas L. Robertson, Ph.D.

Chair, Social Science Department
Director, Human Studies Program
Marylhurst College
Portland, OR

Foreword by William Bridges, Ph.D.

 **ACCELERATED DEVELOPMENT INC.**
Publishers
Muncie   Indiana

Self-Directed

GROWTH

© Copyright 1988 by Accelerated Development Inc.

1 2 3 4 5 6 7 8 9 10

International Standard Book Number: 0-915-202-75-1
Library of Congress Number: 87-72746

Library of Congress Cataloging in Publication Data

Robertson, Douglas L., 1950-
Self-directed growth.

Bibliography: p.
Includes index.
1. Self-actualization (Psychology)   2. Change
(Psychology)   3. Learning, Psychology of.   4. Adulthood
--Psychological aspects.   I. Title.
BF637.S4R58   1988   158'.1   87-72746
ISBN 0-915202-75-1

Printed in the United States of America

Technical Development: Tanya Dalton
                       Marguerite Mader
                       Sheila Sheward

Cover Art: Kay Slusarenko, Lake Oswego, OR

Author's Photograph: Joe Walicki, Lake Oswego, OR

 ACCELERATED DEVELOPMENT Inc., PUBLISHERS
3400 Kilgore Avenue, Muncie, IN 47304
(317) 284-7511

DEDICATION

To all of the lifelong
learners whom I have
known—in appreciation
of their courage,
their wisdom, and
especially, all that
they have taught me.

FOREWORD

by William Bridges, Ph.D.

In *The Change Masters,* Rosabeth Moss Kanter tells about a tribe that discovered the wonders of roast pork when a pig got trapped in a burning hut—and which then ritualized hut-burning as the only way that they could imagine to recreate the experience. Doug Robertson retells this tale in the course of making a point in *Self-Directed Growth,* but the tale has a larger relevance to his message and might, in fact, serve as an epigraph to the book as a whole.

For although people have been engaging in growth-producing endeavors since the beginning of human history, it has not been common until very recently for large groups of adults to undertake them self-consciously. Even today personal growth is too often the painful and expensive by-product of a process that is as unthought out as hut-burning. And not surprisingly, until now there has not been a primer for that undertaking. Doug Robertson has supplied that primer with this most useful book.

Self-Directed Growth is a valuable map to the no-man's land where education, philosophy, adult-development, and counseling meet. This is the trackless waste that we usually encounter when we try to explore the relation between learning and personal meaning. The book helps the student wrestle with issues of identity, knowledge, change, and purpose. Better yet, it does so in a clear sequence of steps that keep the student on track.

With the "average" student today being more and more likely to be beyond the traditional college age, this map of the territory of self-directed learning is long overdue. Too many of its would-be competitors err either by being about "adult education," while leaving out anything for learners themselves, or by being cookbooks full of recipes for how to throw off the past or dive into the future, while leaving out the critical process of learning.

Robertson's book will be used in many ways. Self-directed learners, either inside an educational institution or outside, will use it to launch themselves on journeys of self-discovery. Groups of them, working under the guidance of a mentor, will use it as a text for exciting new kinds of courses. And teachers will use it as a guide to reorienting their own efforts away from implanting content and toward developing students.

Writing before the book is even published, I have no way of foreseeing how it will find its way into the world of adult learners. But I can imagine that it will follow the route taken by underground classics: word of mouth, loans that are never returned, gifts bought by the dozen for one's friends, and purchases by thousands of people who see the book on a shelf and grasp intuitively (and correctly) that this book is talking about them.

I suggest this because, like many such classics, the book is a very human document, written with humor and grace by someone who takes the reader much more seriously than he takes himself. It is full of wonderful quotes from everyone from Heraclitus to Woody Allen—from poetry, from Zen stories, and from the writings of social scientists. It successfully blends theory and practical suggestions without becoming either too abstract or too simplistic. The book is, in the best sense of the word, a *personal* one. It is by a person who has listened carefully to many other people talking about their hopes and their needs. It is based on a thorough knowledge of the studies of such people as students. And it is written by a person who has thought a good deal about his own educational journey.

So what are you doing reading this Foreword? Turn the page and get on with the book itself!

William Bridges, Ph.D.
Mill Valley, California
October, 1987

PREFACE

Something significant is happening. Not so long ago becoming an adult was thought to involve an ending of major growth and transition and a settling into a particular persona and niche for life's duration. Becoming a "grown up" carried a certain finality with it, and stories of full-fledged adults who were exploring themselves and their lifestyle options were met by most folks with wonder, suspicion, and fear, much as were accounts of miracles in medieval times. Of course, this developmental cessation in adulthood has never been completely true, but many people thought that it was.

Nowadays, adulthood is being redefined in our society. The human lifespan has grown to be relatively long in the biological world, and as a culture, we are moving toward the belief that development can occur, and *should* occur, throughout this long journey, rather than just at the beginning. Old habits die hard, but fewer and fewer people are thinking in terms of what they want to do when they "grow up." Instead, we are tending to think about the need to learn to manage life's changes—the undeniable changes which are all around us and within us—and the need to learn to direct our own growth in the midst of these changes.

Expressions of this new belief in lifelong learning and growth are numerous and diverse. One manifestation with which I am especially familiar is the dramatic increase in the number of adults who are returning to school. Indeed, for several years adult students have outnumbered their younger peers on the campuses of the country's more than three thousand colleges and universities (Chickering & Associates, 1981, p. xxvii).

A society's institutions—such as its colleges and universities—exist to serve its population. I am pleased to report that American institutions of higher education are adjusting to accommodate this new student population. Increasingly, adult learners can find educational programs which are suitable for them in terms of flexible degree requirements, acknowledgement of prior learning, adult-oriented learning environments, delivery systems which are convenient for people who work, and so forth. From what I have seen after ten years of working in this field is that excellent prospects exist for the widespread institutionalization of these innovations. A great deal remains to be done, but the foothold is secure.

So, we have some good programmatic alternatives being developed for adult learners. But what about appropriate reading materials for the various courses within these programs? Here I think is a new frontier.

The fact that adults require different teaching strategies than do 18 to 22 year olds is understood by a rapidly growing number of educators. This issue has been the focus of research for well over a decade, and now a substantial literature exists which clearly establishes major differences between adult students and traditional-age students (e.g., Brookfield, 1986; Chickering & Associates, 1981; Cross, 1981; Daloz, 1986; Kidd, 1973; Knowles, 1975, 1980; Knowles & Associates, 1984; Knox, 1977, 1986; and Wlodkowski, 1985).

However, even though we have more programs which feature adult-oriented teaching strategies, we certainly do not have the books to go with the classes. My colleagues and I consistently have trouble finding suitable books for our adult classes. Trade books are usually too thin on theory and research. Professional books are often too technical for undergraduates. Traditional textbooks are generally written for what our adult students call "kids." What we need is a new kind of textbook...for adults...one which is theoretically comprehensive and sound, yet engaging, entertaining, practical, and clearly connected to important adult experiences.

I have tried to write such a book here. This book is written for adults who are interested in learning to manage change constructively. It is designed to be useful as a self-help resource should the learner be working independently. However, it is especially intended to provide a good text for teachers or trainers who are leading credit courses or non-credit workshops on various topics dealing with adult development.

The book presents a good deal of material concerning two important questions: What is development? And how can it be facilitated? The book presents this material in a way which is appropriate for busy, adult learners. The pace is brisk but unhurried. Jargon is held to a minimum, although ideas are not. Practice is combined with theory. And the tone invites the reader to participate all along the way.

As I wrote this book, I imagined the audience to be some of my favorite classes...gatherings in which the people and the climate seemed special and the discussions yielded unexpected and precious insights. I hope that the reader comes away from this book with the sense of having experienced something like those special encounters which I had in mind as I wrote these words.

Douglas L. Robertson, Ph.D.
Lake Oswego, Oregon
August, 1987

TABLE OF CONTENTS

ACKNOWLEDGEMENTS

As we will discuss later, individual achievements are really the result of group efforts. And so it is with this book. A book can be seen to have a "being" which like a person develops in interaction with its environment. Many people, things, and contexts have contributed to this project, and to each of these elements of the book's environment, I extend my deep gratitude for helping with its development.

As we all know, however, some parts of the environment are more critical than others regarding the success of a developmental project. So, in addition, I would like to single out a few people for special thanks.

During the four years of this project, I have enjoyed the monumental support of the Liberal Arts staff at Marylhurst College. I find it difficult to express the degree to which their cheerful competence and commitment have added to my day-to-day security. By explicitly supporting my academic activities with their interest and understanding, and by expertly facilitating my work as a program manager through their savvy handling of the millions of details which our busy office generates, they have added significantly to this project. The team has had many contributing members over the years, and to each of them, I extend appreciation. Deserving of special recognition are the full-time staff during the period in which this book was written. In alphabetical order, they are as follows: Nancy Kuehnel, Beth Prins, Pam Stephens, and Kathryn Stillings. The Liberal Arts team deserves special thanks for all that it has contributed not only to this book but also to establishing, along with many others at Marylhurst College, a viable lifelong learning center in the United States.

The leader of this team is Dr. Janet Bennett, a colleague and friend during my ten-plus years at Marylhurst. Janet is a major figure in the international community of intercultural educators, trainers, and researchers, and a chief architect of many creative and successful innovations in lifelong learning. Yet somehow she found the time to be this book's principle sounding board as it was being written. Janet has a master's ear for the needs and wants of adult learners. And as the draft of each chapter was finished, I would give it to her for a rehearsal. Her feedback and encouragement were not only generous but also essential for this project. Without it, this book would be very different and, I think, much the worse. She models in her daily life a frame of reference which, in my opinion, facilitates the kind of collaborative relationships to which colleagues should aspire. Her approach is a deep commitment on her part; it is very special in professional worlds; and it is much appreciated by me.

In our programs for adult learners at Marylhurst, this team has tried to create a "co-learning" environment—one in which the faculty learns from the students as well as the more conventional relationship in which students learn from the faculty. In my faculty and counselor roles, I have learned an immeasurable amount from the students, and I have tried to express the depth of my gratitutde by dedicating this book to all the lifelong learners whom I have known. In particular, I would like to give special thanks to all of the advisees who have shared their stories with me over the years and to all of the participants in the classes in which many of the ideas for this book were developed, tested, and refined. In very important ways, this is really their book.

Also, regarding the content and approach of this book, I would like to express my appreciation to the various practitioners, researchers, and theorists in the field of adult development and adult learning whom I have encountered along the way. Some of the these people I have met personally and have profited immensely from our conversations. Others I know only through their writings. I am someone who develops a relationship with a "literature," and my relationship with this body of work has been a very satisfying one for me. I am continually impressed not only by how much I learn from professionals in this area but also by how much they inspire me by their learner-centered values and their willingness to tackle difficult, real-world problems. For this fine community, I am grateful.

Access to a community of ideas and practices is difficult without good library services. In a large research university, collections are huge, and you can do much of the library work yourself. In a small, liberal arts college, materials often must be tracked down and borrowed from elsewhere. For this endeavor, you need help. Finding myself in the latter case, I relied heavily on the staff of Marylhurst's Shoen Library in researching this book. I was in good hands. These people—Paula Hamilton, Pierina Parise, Susan Barnes Whyte, and their assistants—consistently amazed me with their sophisticated techniques, their dedication to my project, and their enormous good humor. With humane people such as these, equipped with increasingly powerful computers, I feel much more confident that the "information age" will be a good one.

Also, a word of acknowledgement is due to Kay Slusarenko, the person responsible for the book's cover art. Kay is a public artist of considerable reputation. With twenty commissions to her credit, sh is among the most prolific and highly-respected public artists in the Northwest. Also, she chairs Marylhurst's Art Department, whose programs have a sterling reputation in the art world. As an act of friendship, she reserved time in her demanding schedule in order to do the cover art. I, and the many who will enjoy her creation, owe her a great deal.

In addition, with regard to the visual aspects of the book, I would like to thank Joe Walicki for contributing the author's portrait to the project. Joe is a recruitment counselor at Marylhurst College and, also, a very fine photographer.

Like creating a finished piece of art, producing a book is a complex endeavor, and of course, the publisher is a crucial part of that process. One hears many horror stories from authors about battles, sometimes even wars, with their publishers. With Accelerated Development, my experience has been just the opposite. I think that Dr. Joseph Hollis, President of Accelerated Development, and his associates deserve special recognition for their enlightened attitude toward book publishing. When the relationship begins with Accelerated Development, one receives an authors' manual. Along with technical guidelines, the manual includes a statement of philosophy—a collaborative, facilitative perspective which focuses on development...of the book, the author, the reader, and AD itself. I was impressed by this "mission statement." And as I watched the philosophy lived out in the production of this book, my appreciation grew even more. I think that people need to know about this group—about their hard work but particularly about their collaborative, developmental approach to making books.

Finally, I would like to extend these acknowledgements into the future. The "being" of a book does not stop developing with its publication. Entering print is simply a transition in its journey. From this vantage, we can see that this book's development will continue with its use. For all of you who contribute to this phase of its development—by using, elaborating, and sharing its ideas—I am grateful, much like a parent who appreciates those people who help the child once he or she leaves home.

READERS' COMMENTS

Doug Robertson's *Self-Directed Growth* is a superb resource for both the adult learner and the faculty member or administrator who is fortunate enough to work with the adult learner. *Self-Directed Growth* is informative as well as being helpful. Robertson doesn't talk down to his reader (as was so common in the anti-intellectualism of growth-oriented books in the 1960s and 1970s). He is willing to grapple—successfully—with difficult concepts, such as "change," "growth," and "development," rather than just taking the terms for granted or using them indiscriminantly. Doug Robertson is a true interdisciplinarian in this book. He exhibits, quite gently, an impressive breadth of knowledge—from Abraham Maslow to Michael Polanyi, from William Shakespeare to Carol Gilligan. I will recommend this book to the adult learners in my school, as well as our faculty and staff. I urge others to do the same!

William H. Bergquist, Ph.D.
President, The Professional School of Psychology, San Francisco, California, Author, *Designing Undergraduate Education* and *Planning Effectively For Educational Quality*

In *Self-Directed Growth*, Doug Robertson has created one of the "moons which light up our dark nights" and assisted us in answering the often-heard question, "But what do I do on Monday morning?"

This wonderfully readable, practical, theoretically sound and poetic book will help *all* adults—whether they define themselves as teacher or learner—to better understand and use both other's theories and their own experience as they develop their unique styles in the "art of growing."

Robertson has successfully integrated the universal and ageless themes of "self, other, and society," as he carefully weaves the story of developmental growth.

During the more than thirty years during which I have sought the answers to "How do people learn?" and "How do institutions change?", I have often wished that a book such as *Self-directed Growth* was available. Now that it is, I want to immediately rush out to get copies for the thousands of adult students and adult educators with whom I work.

Self-Directed Growth is required reading for every adult-learner, teacher, manager, worker who has become addicted, as I have, to the marvelous, mysterious phenomenon that we call learning.

Doug Robertson has made a significant contribution to the new and expanding literature on adult learning. We should all be grateful for the opportunity he has given us to broaden and deepen the important conversation about adult developmental growth.

Elinor M. Greenberg, Ed.D.

Regional Executive Office and Program Administrator, PATHWAYS To The Future: A joint venture between Mountain Bell, the Communication Workers of America and CAEL, The Council for Adult and Experiential Learning

This very special book calls for a new approach to knowing, one that relates the knower to the known and integrates self and world. *Self-Directed Growth*, builds on Doug Robertson's solid experience with adult learners and reflects his commitment to and deep respect for adult men and women who are willing to take responsibility for their own making of meaning. The writing of this book has been enriched by Robertson's unusual capacity to listen and learn from his adult students. He relates intellectual substance to concrete, lived experience. Rich theoretical discussions are tied to the contexts, conditions, and struggles with life that foster adult learning and growth. In *Self-Directed Growth*, adult students now have a guide to assist them in the cultivation of one of life's most valuable capacities, learning to learn.

R. Eugene Rice, Ph.D.
Professor and Chair, Department of Sociology, University of the Pacific, and Senior Fellow, Carnegie Foundation for the Advancement of Teaching (Princeton), 1988-1989.

.

CHAPTER 1

GETTING STARTED

Luck is a crossroad where preparation and opportunity meet.

Anoñymous

This is a book about learning to create this kind of luck. Our topic is how to prepare ourselves, and how to manage our worlds, so that we consistently find opportunity rather than oppression, growth rather than stagnation. Our focus is on change—chosen or unchosen—and how to help it to lead to development.

This book is not just another rallying call for personal growth, nor is it yet another cookbook for personal success, although it is long on both enthusiasm and straightforward suggestions. Certainly a place exists for each kind of book. However, I am seeking a deeper empowerment here.

My aim is to increase our proficiency at directing our own development. In order to do this, we must not only be *inspired*...we must also be *informed.* We must go beyond doing merely *what we are told*...we also must *understand what to do.* In short, we must have our own well-founded theory of development and be able to apply it in new situations to whatever developmental project on which we may be working. Large or small, personal or professional, chosen or unchosen, all of our growth projects can benefit remarkably from a good theory of development...if we have one. This book will help to generate such a theory.

Noted psychologist Kurt Lewin once wrote, "...there is nothing so practical as a good theory" (Lewin, 1951, p. 169). I firmly believe this. Having an understanding of the process in which we are involved helps us to move through that process more productively and satisfyingly, just as having a good map empowers us to find our way more easily. Theory and practice, like the left and right brains of the fully functioning person, are best developed in integration. And so it will be in this book...theory and practice in interdependent relationship.

OBJECTIVES

Influential theorist Ervin Goffman, in attempting to crystalize his perspective on human experience, wrote that his work essentially focused on a single issue: how individuals go about answering the question, "What is it that's going on here?" (Goffman, 1974, p. 8). As you begin this book, let me assist you in answering this basic question by briefly discussing my objectives.

In our time together, I want to do three things:

1. Generate in each of us a clear and easily applied framework for development,

2. Explore ten specific features in ourselves and in our worlds which promote development, and

3. Improve our skills at actualizing these features in our day-to-day living.

Objective One: A Framework for Development

The first objective is critical for any growth project: we must know what development is. From our conception of growth comes our specific developmental goals in any particular situation. And from these goals come our specific strategies.

When asked what time is, St. Augustine replied, "I know, but when you ask me I don't" (Watts, 1951, p. 55). For many of us, this would be our response to the question, "What is growth?" While this is a perfectly understandable answer—after all, the question is a difficult one—this approach does have its limitations.

The philosopher Michael Polanyi made an insightful distinction between "tacit knowledge"—the silent, intuitive kind which comprises things which we "just know"—and "articulate knowledge"—the rational kind which we can verbalize and explain (Polanyi, 1962). He pointed out, quite perceptively, that we know far more than we can say (Polanyi, 1966, p. 4).

While this may be true, conscious planning to facilitate our own development, or the development of others, is made difficult if our knowledge of development is only "tacit." Structuring a definition of growth does not mean that we need to lose a "feel" for it, as we may sometimes fear. It simply means that we have a critical basis on which to formulate clear and effective goals—those which help us to organize our activities in truly constructive ways. Our work on the first objective—to create a conscious and well-organized framework for development—will not strip growth of its beauty, magic, and serendipity. Instead, it should make this kind of special experience more likely.

**Objectives Two and Three:
Identifying and Enhancing
Conditions which Promote Development**

Whereas the first objective involves creating a basis for *goal setting,* the second and third objectives—exploring conditions which promote development—relate to learning to create effective *strategies* and *resources* in order to achieve these goals. Enough is known about the developmental process that we can identify some specific features—within ourselves and within our everyday worlds—which seem to foster growth. These features provide us with an initial checklist to consider as we go about formulating our various growth projects.

LOOKING AHEAD

So much for the objectives of this book...how do I plan to achieve them? The approach will be fairly straightforward, as an overview of the book's three parts will indicate.

**Part I: Answering the Question,
"What is Development?"**

In Part I, we will work on the first objective by exploring a framework for development. We will begin by making a distinction between *development-as-change* and *development-as-growth,* making clear that this book is about *growth.* Then, we will examine a few basic principles from *systems theory* as a means of acquiring some key concepts with which to understand development-as-growth. Next, we will discuss a useful way of thinking about that which we are trying to develop—human beings. We will talk about the person as an integrated system of *content and process.* Development will then be defined as the *transformation of the person,* either as a whole or in terms of specific content or process aspects. Following this exploration of the nature of development, we will investigate *development's various phases,* or those periods in the transition process which William Bridges has aptly termed "endings," "the neutral zone," and "new beginnings" (Bridges, 1980). In Part I, by improving our understanding of what development is and the course which development typically follows, we will increase our ability to formulate our developmental goals and to anticipate problems which may arise, regardless of the specific situation.

Parts II and III: Answering the Question, "What Can the Environment and the Person Contribute to Development?"

In Parts II and III, we will deal with strategies and resources for achieving our developmental goals. These sections will deal with the book's second and third objectives—identifying factors which promote growth and enhancing their presence in our daily lives.

Our growth, whether personal or professional, all-encompassing or relatively narrow, can be seen to result from the interaction of two sets of factors: those having to do with our *environments,* and those having to do with *ourselves.* In Part II, we will explore five characteristics of the environment which tend to promote development: *novelty, minimal threat, supportiveness of the learning cycle, information richness,* and *learning facilitators.* In Part III, we will examine five features of the person which contribute to development: *self-awareness, growth motivation, learning skills, knowledge of the developmental process,* and *developmental planning.* The reasons why these characteristics of environments and of ourselves tend to encourage development will be discussed in some detail, along with ways in which we can enhance each of the ten features in our specific growth projects.

SOURCES OF LEARNING

In this book, I have synthesized learning on change and growth which has come from several sources. One source is the last ten years of studying the existing theory and research on adult development. A second source is a decade of serving as a teacher, counselor, and program manager in a special part of the world called the Liberal Arts Division, an innovative, exciting, and very effective set of adult learning programs at Marylhurst College, in Portland, Oregon.

Through this work, I have learned that adult students typically re-enter school because of a trigger event which has catapulted them into transition (Aslanian & Brickell, 1980). A spouse's death, a job loss, an empty nest, a health loss, a divorce...whatever the specific event might be, *re-entry adult students frequently find themselves needing to create a new self for a new world forged by transition.* They usually enter or re-enter college programs not necessarily needing a degree, but much more importantly, also needing to meet some critical developmental challenge.

During my years in the Liberal Arts Division, I have had the privilege of sharing intimately in the developmental struggles of several thousand adults, ranging in age from young-adult to elderly. I have been able to watch these people's courageous transformations from a counselor's and teacher's vantage, and I have tried to understand the process which was unfolding before my eyes. I also have had the opportunity to try out various ways of facilitating these developmental transformations, rather than forcing or just ignoring them. This first-hand experience, along with a careful study of the scholarly literature on adult development, forms the basis for this book...at least much of the basis, anyway.

My own journey also plays a major role in this synthesis. Helping my father to die an early death from cancer, participating in the peaceful dissolution of a marriage, changing careers, living and working in another culture...each of these events—sometimes excruciatingly and sometimes exhilaratingly—has triggered a significant transition in me. I always have tried to learn and to grow from these changes, not merely to endure them. This learning, too, is an important part of this book

PROACTIVITY VS. REACTIVITY

As we get started, a key concept which informs my frame of reference needs to be explained. Underlying this book's objectives and overall perspective is the value of *proactivity.* The idea has fundamental significance in a world of rapid change and perhaps can best be understood in contrast to its opposite—*reactivity.*

Proactive Perspective

Proactivity has several key features. To begin, the proactive perspective recognizes that change is constant, and that we are involved in its process, no matter how powerful we become, either personally or through our allegiances. With wisdom, we come to realize and accept this bond, as this Zen story illustrates:

> Once when Hyakujo delivered some Zen lectures an old man attended them, unseen by the monks. At the end of each talk when the monks left so did he. But one day he remained after they had gone, and Hyakujo asked him: "Who are you?"
>
> The old man replied: "I am not a human being, but I was a human being when the Kashapa Buddha preached in this world. I was a Zen master and lived on this mountain. At that time one of my students asked me whether or not the enlightened man is subject to the law of causation. I answered him: 'The enlightened man is not subject to the law of causation.' For this answer evidencing a clinging to absoluteness I became a fox for five hundred rebirths, and I am still a fox. Will you save me from this condition with your Zen words and let me get out of a fox's body? Now may I ask you: Is the enlightened man subject to the law of causation?"
>
> Hyakujo said: "The enlightened man is one with the law of causation."
>
> At the words of Hyakujo the old man was enlightened. (Reps, 1957, p. 96)

While change may be constant, it is not random. A "law of causation" does exist. The present in which we live is related in an important way to our past, just as the future in which we will live will evolve from our present. Assuming a proactive perspective simply acknowledges this connectedness of events and places a premium on participating actively, yet humbly, in the change process.

Of course, our present actions do not rigidly *determine* how we will be in the future. For one thing, the change process is complex, and we are only one participant in it. And for another thing, *choice* seems to be an essential feature of human existence. We are always constructing our present through our choices.

However, even though the present does not determine our future, it does seem to shape the range of possibilities from which we have to choose. We are neither totally free agents who are able, with a little "positive thinking," to leap tall buildings in a single bound, nor are we preconditioned automotons who respond predictably to every stimulus. We are something in between superbeings and robots, making choices among options which we ourselves have helped to create. Being proactive simply means that we take responsibility for our power to create our options, while being fully aware that our power is not absolute. We seemingly acknowledge that at every moment we are laying groundwork for the next moment. Thus we accept that we are all agents of change, whether we like it or not.

Reactive Perspective

In contrast, the *reactive* perspective tends to see us as separate from the dynamics of change. From this point of view, change is something *to which we react*, not some all-embracing process *of which we are a part*. The reactive frame of reference fragments and reifies change into specific events, as in, "this change" or "that change." We are seen to respond to these external events, and either maintain the status quo, or not. If we do not, crisis ensues. In the reactive frame, crisis precipitates innovation, rather than ongoing planning. And consequently, pain—rather than pleasure—comes to be associated with transition. For these reasons, the reactive person, in contrast to the proactive person, not only feels more alienated from the world, but also adapts more slowly and finds adaptation painful. Life requires adaptation, and because adaptation is painful to the reactive person, life itself becomes painful.

Proactivity: An Essential Survival Skill

Feeling especially stressed one day, a friend of mine joked that he was about to become evolution's next victim. Admiring his sense of humor in a pinch, I laughed and asked him what he meant. He explained with a twinkle that he believed rapid change to be the next environmental stress which would cause an evolutionary shift in the human species: those who could learn to adapt to rapid change successfully and satisfyingly would tend to survive and pass along their genes, and those who could not—himself foremost among them—would not be so lucky.

Even though he was joking, my friend may be right about the critical significance of learning to adapt. If he is, those people with a proactive perspective appear to be the ones who will have the "luck" in upcoming years. On one level, this book may be about learning to succeed at specific developmental projects, but even more deeply, it is about learning the practice of proactivity, perhaps the most fundamental and important developmental skill

STRIVING IN SERVICE...SERVICE IN STRIVING

Oliver Wendell Homes once said, "There is nothing so commonplace as the wish to be remarkable." While this statement serves as a warning of the hubris in us all, nonetheless, I find it to be a profoundly encouraging description of human beings. The portrayal implies a vitality and an orientation toward improvement which somehow seems healthy.

While studying Zen Buddhism, I used to be intrigued by how hard I was striving not to strive. The teachings held that desire was the source of suffering, and here I was desiring with all my might not to desire. The situation puzzled me. Eventually, I learned that striving comes in many forms and that while some forms may be destructive (or at least, *get in* the way), others are quite constructive (or *pave* the way). In my view, our desire to be remarkable, our desire to achieve our unique potentialities, can be a very constructive striving, depending on the purposes which motivate us...for example, self-aggrandizement vs. service.

This book will provide some maps and vehicles for this enterprise of making our way toward growth. My hope is that this journey is motivated by the desire to serve something larger than the self and that the power of this growth will be used wisely and with love.

PART I

WHAT IS DEVELOPMENT?

The issue is one of choice, and choice is always a question of alternatives. ....To claim that intelligence is a better method than its alternatives, authority, imitation, caprice and ignorance, prejudice and passion, is hardly an excessive claim.

John Dewey, *Experience and Nature* (1958, p. 437)

Thoughts without content are empty
Intuitions without concepts are blind.

Immanuel Kant (Kolb, 1984, p. 106)

What is development? This question is important for at least two reasons. First, unless we have a reasonably lucid and well-informed answer to this question, then as we try to develop ourselves and others, quite simply, we do not know what we are doing. This situation makes formulating effective developmental strategies rather difficult. And not knowing *what* we are doing, nor *how* we plan to do it, puts knowing *when* we have done it out of the question. A good first step toward learning to actualize significant developmental projects consistently is to have an articulate conception of development.

The second benefit of having a good theory of development is that this conceptual framework provides us with a basis for intervening constructively in groups of people as well as in individual lives. As we will discover in the upcoming sections on systems theory, striking parallels exist between the ways in which individuals and groups develop. For those of us who have either a personal or professional interest in helping groups—such as families, work units, organizations, communities, or whole societies—to achieve higher levels of organization and competence, this work on formulating a definition of development will be an extremely wise investment of time and energy.

In the next five chapters, we will work up to, and then explore, a theory of development. Chapters 2, 3, and 4 will provide important background for our exploration. In Chapter 2, we will look at the difference between *development-as-change* and *development-as-growth;* in Chapter 3, we will examine some fundamental principles of *systems theory;* and in Chapter 4, we will establish a way of thinking about the person as a combination of *process and content.* In Chapter 5, we will come to the heart of the matter by investigating a *definition of development.* And in Chapter 6, we will round out the exploration by looking at *development's characteristic phases.*

Objective for Part I: To generate a clear and easily applied framework for development.

CHAPTER **2**

GROWTH VS. CHANGE

And on her lover's arm she leant
And round her waist she felt it fold,
And far across the hills they went
In that new world which is the old.

Alfred, Lord Tennyson,
The Day Dream (1899a, p. 132)

Love transformed their worlds—this woman's and this man's. Growth has a similar effect on each of us, as we will see. Growth is not just change; it is transformation. But before we discuss growth, let's experience it. Good concepts—ones which we can trust enough to use—come from experience, not the other way around.

GROWTH EXPERIENCES

If you like to learn through concrete experience, you will enjoy the upcoming exercise. If you prefer to learn through the discussion of abstract concepts, you may find the exercise a bit difficult. Try to stretch a little. You will find the time well spent. The abstractions from experience will come soon, but first comes the experience.

Visualizing Growth

To begin, we will explore some very special home movies. Find a quiet place, and think back over your life. Try to identify some periods when you felt that you really grew, really expanded yourself. Then, pick one of those periods which you would like to spend some time re-experiencing.

Perhaps your growth experience had to do with your *whole personhood,* a time when you felt that you went through a major shift in your overall maturity, when you felt that you became an entirely new and better person. Or perhaps the experience focused on some *part of you,* such as your ability to parent your children, to manage your work, or to resolve intimacy's inevitable conflict between a healthy self-love and the deep love of another. Perhaps your growth experience involved sensing the connection between your own physical health and your mental states, a realization which sparked in you a significantly different interest in nutrition and exercise. Perhaps the experience had to do with a time when you felt that you took responsibility for your own faith, instead of simply following the prescriptions of authority figures.

Maybe the experience which you select involved growth which was professionally oriented, such as a time when you felt that you finally understood how your organization worked, or perhaps how organizations in general work. Perhaps the experience dealt with your realization of just what it means for a society to pass from an industrial age to an information age, and of how you and your career fit into that transformation. Perhaps the growth experience involved feeling that you finally fathomed the meaning of computer technology, and could see just what it was that you needed to know and what you did not need to know, just what you needed to buy and what you did not need to buy.

Whatever the nature of the growth experience which you choose—whether large or small, personal or professional—get a fix on that period of your life and let your mind re-experience it. Try to picture the contexts of the experience. Where did it take place? What did you look like then? Who else was involved? What did they look like? What were some of the really important scenes? Re-live them if you can. What were your thoughts at the time? What were your feelings? What did you do? How about the other people? What did they think, feel, and do? As you approached your growth and then passed through it, what were the changes in what you thought, felt, and did? How about those around you? What were the things which prompted your change? What were the consequences of your growth?

As you feel ready—as you feel some kind of completeness to your re-living of these experiences—take a few moments to record the significant features of your home movie. Jot down the major characters, the plot, the scenes, the action, and especially the character development. *Try to lay the experiential groundwork for formulating some generalizations about what happened to you as you grew.*

Examples of Growth Experiences

Here are some examples of what other people have said when asked to reflect on their growth experiences. Not long ago, I had the privilege of meeting a man who told me this story about himself. He was in his late forties and was a tenured professor at a small, liberal arts college in the upper Midwest. He had had modest career ambitions, but even so, like most people his achievements were somewhat less than what he had intended. He felt that he was on the other side of his professional life, and the grass was not greener as he thought that it would be. Family had always been important to him, but now, even more so. In his family, he was husband, father, breadwinner; he was central. *His* professional life was the *family's* professional life. Or at least that is the way that it used to be, he felt. His wife had gone back to school, first to earn her baccalaureate degree, and eventually, a doctorate. But she did not just complete her programs satisfactorily. She whizzed through them with flying colors and was offered a teaching job at a large, state university, a far more prestigious school than his own. Meanwhile, their children were getting older and were beginning to move away from home. All at once, he felt that he was losing his potency in his work and in his family. Both he and his wife were in therapy trying to sort things out, but he admitted that he was having the most trouble. He believed in family, and he felt that he needed it desperately right now. Yet his family's form was unclear, unstable, in transition. What he went on to describe was a new perspective which he was forming about himself and his world. No longer defining himself simply in terms of the roles which he filled, he was adding to those changing role characteristics a deeper awareness of his unique strengths and weaknesses as an individual. Along with this more developed self-concept, he was coming to realize that families, as well as individuals, can come in many forms. Most importantly, he was becoming genuinely comfortable with these new forms, instead of negatively evaluating anything which departed from the straight and narrow, Dad-wears-the-pants-in-the-family conceptions of manhood and home life. He felt that a period of profound disorientation was ending, and that a new and better, more adaptable, life structure was emerging. He confessed that periodically he still grieved over the loss of his former self and world, but he added with stunning sincerity that he would not go back for anything. He had passed through the dark night, and the morning had never looked better to him.

Another story of growth recounted to me went like this. A woman in her early forties told of how her life had been shattered when she had discovered a few years earlier that her husband had had an affair. Although her life had felt a little bland and like a grind at times, she had bought the idea of the traditional nuclear family and was reasonably happy in her roles of wife and mother. With the knowledge of her husband's affair, however, her life structure caved in on her. She was attractive, but she felt dumpy. She was intelligent, but she felt stupid. She had a talent for insight, but she felt foolish. She normally had great zest, but she felt exhausted. Her organizational skills were legendary among her friends and family, but suddenly she felt overwhelmed by chaos. Anger, confusion, anxiety, depression prevailed. She could not go back to the way things were. Never again. And then, slowly, she and her husband rebuilt a "second marriage." She went back to school in order to begin a career in human services. She vowed never to be caught without the capacity to earn a meaningful living on her own. Her husband understood this need, and supported her. She did well, and went on to graduate school. Now, she has embarked on an excellent career in counseling. Her children have a new mother, someone who parents rather than is a "parent." And her husband has a new partner, an individual with whom he relates intimately rather than someone who is a "wife." She too has new children and a new husband as a result. Her expression held a poignant complexity as she told me her story. And tears fell. The transformation of self and world was painful. But a quiet, sure smile at the story's end made me believe her when she said that it had been worth it.

Let's look at one more example of a growth experience, this one coming from professional life. A faculty member told of becoming a department chairperson and suddenly realizing his management inadequacies. Trained to be thorough, precise, and above all dispassionate in his scholarly pursuits, he found that he took too long to make decisions and that *esprit de corps* around the department was vanishing rapidly. He seemed to upset people, and he did not understand why. His accustomed style of processing information and communicating with others, things at which he excelled in the study and in the seminar room, no longer worked in the chairperson's office. He told of his eroding confidence and of how he dreaded coming to work during this period. But he stuck it out, and tried to build a new, more effective perspective. He had good friends who gave him support and solid advice, and he set out on an important new learning project to become a better chairperson. He read voraciously on the topic, attended conferences, and discreetly interviewed anyone whom he thought could help him, trying not to let anyone know how panicked he was. Then, it all came together for him when he encountered the following passage from George Keller's *Academic Strategy:*

> Administrators tend to be cool, amiably neutral, businesslike; managers tend to be spirited, committed, entrepreneurial. Administrators are usually cautious, passive, and conservative; managers are often risk-takers, active, and adventurous. Administrators love details and efficiency; managers love large objectives and effectiveness.... Thus, the change to a greater future orientation and sharper management in education requires a willed shift in the psyche, a new courage to be, to do. (Keller, 1983, p. 68)

These words crystallized for him what he had come to know vaguely somewhere deep inside of himself: he was an "administrator" who wanted, and needed, to learn to be a "manager." His objectives became clear to him, and he went on to make excellent progress toward achieving them. In the process, he added a new dimension to his personality, and he felt like a new, more competent person.

New, more competent, transformed...growth seems to involve a sense of transformation...of ourselves and our worlds, like Tennyson's lovers in the beginning of this chapter. Think of your own growth experiences. Did their resolution leave you with a feeling of being a new person? If not your whole person, then did some part of you feel new? As a new person who looked at things differently, did the world around you also seem transformed in some significant way? Did many of your relationships somehow seem new? To these questions, most people answer, "Yes."

SIMPLE CHANGE EXPERIENCES

Now let's explore another kind of experience. Well over a hundred years ago, Alphonse Karr coined what has become a common French expression, *"Plus ça change, plus c'est la même chose,"* which means, "The more things change, the more they stay the same" (Karr, 1849). This phrase captures that sense which we sometimes have of encountering change in our lives, perhaps even dramatic change, *without* an accompanying sense of significant transformation of ourselves or the way in which we look at the world. Paradoxically, these experiences involve newness which does not seem new.

Visualizing Simple Change

For the second movie of our double feature, each of us needs to select one of these situations from our past which we would be willing, and able, to re-experience. The situation which you select might have involved moving to a new city, or perhaps taking a new job. It might have related to getting married, or divorced. Perhaps it dealt with having another child, or perhaps having had the last child leave home. Or maybe it involved getting a promotion, or retiring. Perhaps it had to do with the death of a parent. Or maybe, it dealt with changing churches. Whatever the experience you choose, it should have involved some situation in which you encountered significant change, but without a sense of experiencing significant growth. Be nice to yourself: don't pick an especially painful situation, unless you have someone to give you support after the exercise.

Once again, find a quiet place and re-live the experience. Try to be concrete in your memories. To get started, visualize an important scene from that period in your life. What did you look like? Who else was involved? What did they look like? Let your mind's eye roam from scene to scene. Don't worry about the chronological order. What were you thinking in each scene? And feeling? And doing? What were the people around you thinking, feeling, and doing? What seemed to change? What stayed the same?

As we did before, when you feel a sense of completeness to the re-experiencing of these events, gather yourself and your observations. Record some notes so that we can compare our two movies. Major characters? Plot? Scenes? Action? Character development? Summarize your second movie.

Examples of Simple Change Experiences

Here is how one woman described this kind of experience to me. She told of a period in her early thirties when she had felt a vague but deep dissatisfaction with the way in which her life was going. She had married in her early twenties, and with two children coming soon after, she had immersed herself in being a good wife and mother. She knew right away that something was missing, but since she did not know exactly what it was, she told herself to keep still and grow up. She lived what Henry David Thoreau called a life of "quiet desperation" (1964, p. 263). She found herself longing for change, any change, hoping that it would provide the magic which would put things straight and let her see what she wanted, and needed. The story which she told involved her family's move from Portland, Oregon, to Houston, Texas, a re-location which was related to her husband's promotion and transfer. The change was immense, and not all bad. Getting to know a new city and region caused her stress, but also her husband's advancement afforded her some new and very desirable luxuries. But she did not find pleasure in these amenities. Somehow, the situation seemed like more of the same. And for a number of years, she had known that the same was not what she needed. Change, but no change...the situation confused her, and she wondered if she would ever be happy. Later, she discovered that she had a strong need to develop a professional life of her own. She had always had this dream, but with her marriage, she had repressed it. Her artistic talent was exceptional and provided great meaning in her life. As she went back to art school and became a practicing artist, she discovered that she and her world were transformed in a significant and growthful way. All of the previous moves—new houses, new cities, new friends, new organizations—had involved change, but not growth.

Perhaps your experience dealt with a professional change, a situation in which you had to fit into a new company but not into a new type of work. The details of your environment were dramatically different—new location, new associates, new bosses—and your adjustments were considerable. But what you had to do to succeed had not changed. No substantial transformation of yourself was required. In fact, transformation was discouraged, since you had been hired as a known commodity who was expected to remain constant and predictable. After the winds settled from the superficial adjustments and a successful maneuvering of the usual probation period, a cloud of sameness—comforting or oppressive, depending on your job satisfaction—re-established itself around you. Change, but no change.

Or perhaps your experience involved a period of longer duration. One man in his mid-thirties told me of how in his early twenties he had been bitterly disappointed in his intimate relationships. He was bright, articulate, dynamic, and as a young man had had outstanding potential in a number of career areas. As a result of his disappointments in his relationships, he had thrown the full power of his commitment into his professional development. He had gone on to establish the beginnings of a very promising career. He had had relationships with women along the way, but committing himself totally to one woman was not something he could do, even in cases where he had wanted desperately to make such a commitment. Intimate relationships terrified him. Many changes had marked his life in the last fifteen years, but somehow his pattern of intimacy—and its limits—had been set for him. Change, but no change. Only when he met a woman who recognized this pattern and who patiently worked with him on issues of intimacy did he begin to feel a transformation in himself, a real growth in his ability to love.

GROWTH VS. SIMPLE CHANGE

The point which emerges from these two sets of experiences is simple. Yet it is often overlooked. *While growth always involves change, not all change results in growth.* Later, we will develop in greater detail just what we mean by growth, but what is suffice to say at this point is that growth involves some kind of significant transformation of the self and usually, as a consequence, of our worlds. Growth is really a subcategory of change, a special kind of change.

Words can be like tail winds which lead us briskly to understanding, or like strong crosswinds which blow us off course. So, let's be careful here in making the meaning of our terms clear. For simplicity's sake, change which does not necessarily result in some kind of important transformation of the self, or some major part of it, we will call "simple change." Change which is somehow importantly transformative of the self, we will call "growth." Incidentally, in the literature on systemic change, these two varieties of change are sometimes called "first-order" and "second-order" change respectively (Watzlawick, Weakland, & Fisch, 1974), but we will stick to our nomenclature here.

Making this distinction between growth and simple change is very useful for us in planning and achieving our own development. Often, people make elaborate plans to create change in their lives, not just for the sake of variety, but hoping to achieve growth. *Focusing on growth from the beginning, rather than on the more general category of change, reduces the hit-and-miss quality of our developmental projects. It helps us to concentrate on what we are really trying to do, and therefore, helps us to do it more effectively.*

During the late 1970s and early 1980s, a good deal of scholarly work was done on the topic of adult development (e.g., Erikson, 1978; Fowler, 1981; Gilligan, 1982; Gould, 1978; Havighurst, 1972; Heath, 1977; Kegan, 1982; Kohlberg, Levine, & Hewer, 1983; D. Levinson, Darrow, Klein, M. Levinson, & McKee, 1978; Loevinger & Blasi, 1976; Lowenthal, Thurnher, & Chiriboga, 1975; McGuigan, 1980; Neugarten, 1968; Perry, 1970; Smelser & Erikson, 1980; Vaillant, 1977). Should you choose to explore this literature, good reviews already exist and need not be duplicated here (e.g., Knefelkamp, Widick, & Parker, 1978; Schlossberg, 1984, pp. 1-40; Weathersby & Tarule, 1980). What you will find in this literature is that the different works focus in varying degrees on the two subcategories of change which we have previously defined: growth and simple change (especially age-related, role transitions). What can become confusing is that all of this diverse research operates under the single heading of development. I would like to avoid any confusion by making our focus explicit here.

In this book, we approach development as a transformation of the self toward increasing life-competence, rather than more generally as an unfolding of changes in life's circumstances and our roles within those circumstances. We all know that a person can go through a whole lifetime of negotiating the changes inherent in leaving home, settling down, raising a family, and retiring, and still not have grown very much. Our concern here involves those times in our lives when we felt that we have really grown—when we felt that our personalities were transformed toward becoming significantly more *complex*, more *flexible*, and more *stable* (Werner, 1948). We want to understand what happened, and how we can intervene in our own lives in order to help it to happen on-call. More than just being change-agents, we want to learn to be growth-agents.

CHAPTER **3**

HEAPS AND WHOLES

No man is an island, entire of itself; every man is a piece of the continent, a part of the main. If a clod be washed away by the sea, Europe is the less, as well as if a promontory were, as well as if a manor of thy friend's or of thine own were: any man's death diminishes me, because I am involved in mankind, and therefore never send to know for whom the bell tolls; it tolls for thee.

John Donne, *Devotions upon Emergent Occasions*
(1959, pp. 108-09).

A large part of being a successful growth-agent is having an effective perspective on ourselves and on our worlds. Behavioral cookbooks may have some short-term utility, but when the conditions or ingredients of our lives change, simple behavioral recipes may not work anymore. At such times, we need to make creative interventions. These kinds of innovations come from the insight provided by our perspectives.

In this chapter, we will briefly introduce the concept of perspective. Then, we will spend a good deal of time exploring one particularly useful perspective—that of systems theory. As we will see from investigating this philosophy of fundamental interconnectedness, growth-agents benefit immensely from remembering that no person, nor any part of a person, is an isolated entity, but rather, as John Donne put it, each is "a part of a main."

PERSPECTIVES

Sometimes called a "world view" or "frame of reference," a perspective is the framework which allows us to construe and process our realities. It gives shape, meaning, emotional color, and direction to our lives. It incorporates our *beliefs* (what we think is real and true), our *attitudes* (how we tend to feel and act toward what we think is real and true), and our *values* (what we think ought to be real and true).

Here's an anonymous riddle which illustrates how our perspectives operate to shape our worlds. After reading the riddle, try to answer it before reading further.

> A man and his only son were going fishing when their car hit some gravel and plunged over an embankment. The man was killed instantly, but the boy was still alive and was found several hours later by some picnickers. They managed to get him to a hospital but he was in perilous condition. He needed immediate attention.
>
> As attendants wheeled the unconscious boy into the emergency room, the doctor on duty looked at him and said, "I can't operate on this boy...he's my son!"
>
> How can this be?

Most people get stuck with this question...at least for a while. How can it be? Here's how: the doctor is a woman; the boy is her son; and the deceased man is her husband. Simple, right? Not really, if our perspective leads us to see doctors as being male.

Our perspective makes this riddle easy or difficult. Likewise, our perspective can make growth easy or difficult. As we go about developing specific growth skills, we must give attention to the overall frame of reference from which these skills emerge. As we develop an effective perspective ourselves, we become empowered to create effective responses on our own regardless of the situation.

SYSTEMS PERSPECTIVE

In recent years, a certain perspective has gained broad influence for its ability to "unstick" people and to help them to operate more effectively in a wide variety of contexts—whether personal or professional, local or global. Called the systems perspective, the approach has several fundamental concepts and principles which will help us a great deal in our own development as growth-agents. A useful statement of the systems perspective can be found in Ervin Laszlo's *Introduction to Systems Philosophy* (1972a). Also helpful, and lighter reading, are the following essays by some of the field's leading theorists: *Mind and Nature,* by Gregory Bateson (1979); *Robots, Men, and Minds,* by Ludwig von Bertalanffy (1967); *The Image,* by Kenneth Boulding (1956); *The Systems View of the World,* by Ervin Laszlo (1972b); and

The Human Use of Human Beings, by Norbert Wiener (1967). In the remainder of this chapter, we will explore some of the basic ideas of systems theory and relate them to our concern with personal and professional development.

Systems as Ordered Wholes

First and foremost is the concept of the system. Before talking about a system in the abstract, however, we should try to experience the concept. Imagine that all of the materials which are necessary to build a house were to be thrown together randomly into an enormous pile: pipes, lumber, nails, wires—all of several different types and sizes—shingles, linoleum, carpet, and gallons of paint; doors and sheets of glass; hinges and sinks; window latches and paneling; and so forth. Imagine all of these things, and lots of others, all heaped together into a gigantic hodgepodge.

Now imagine that some skilled builders wade into this pile and begin the arduous task of sorting out the materials so that they can construct a house. After a considerable amount of effort, and not a little cursing, they organize the materials and begin construction. They have built many houses before and have a general procedure in mind. Their activities for this particular house are directed and coordinated by its blueprint, a plan created from the organizing vision of an architect. Very quickly, they succeed at their second task, and a house appears. From what had been thoroughly disordered, they have created order. But they also have done something more. Earlier, they had created order simply by sorting all of the materials. They did not stop there, however. They went on to put the materials together in a certain way. From this putting-together (or synthesis) came a new entity (a house) which was somehow greater than the simple sum of all of its parts, somehow greater than all the lumber, wires, pipes, glass, and hardware, no matter how neatly arranged. From what had been a disordered heap, they have made an *ordered whole,* or a *system.*

Potential Applications

One of the interesting features of the system concept is that it can refer to any ordered whole, regardless of the type or size of the entity which is involved. For example, an atom is a system, and so is the universe. Walden Pond is a system, just as is the Empire State

Building. The United States is a system, and so is the Amazon Basin. Your family is a system. Even the ideas which inform this book are a system. Anything—whether material or cognitive, natural or social—whose parts are organized to form an entity which is something more than just the sum of these parts is a system.

Boundaries

Systems can be said to have boundaries which separate them from their environments. For example, our house has its walls, roof, and foundation. A system's boundaries need not be literal, however. For example, what is the boundary which separates a family from its environment? Blood lines and legal definitions? Or, how about an attitude system...what are its boundaries? "Boundary" is a broad concept which in its application is sometimes literal and sometimes metaphorical, sometimes precise and sometimes fuzzy. The important feature of a boundary is that it somehow defines—whether loosely or strictly—where the whole stops and the outside begins.

Open and Closed Systems

If a system's boundaries are impermeable, the system is said to be *closed.* Nothing comes in, and nothing goes out. This condition is very rare. More commonly, the boundaries are permeable, and the system is called *open.* In this case, the system has exchanges with its environment. Our house is an open system. For example, it takes in air from the outside and heats or cools that air in order to maintain a certain temperature which we programmed for it when we set the thermostat.

Relationships with the Environment

Whether open or closed, a system has a relationship with its environment—openness and closedness each being a type of relationship. However, in open systems the environment has far greater opportunity to influence the entity through its permeable boundaries. The system must adapt to inputs from the environment so that it can survive as an ordered whole.

The kinds of systems with which we deal in this book—primarily human individuals, groups, and organizations—are open systems. So, the ways in which open systems interact with their environments has special importance for us. Changing the nature of our personality systems can usually be seen to lie at the heart of growth, and as we will see in Part II, managing our environments can play a powerful role in helping to produce this particular kind of systemic change.

Basic Orientations of Systems

Considerable debate has existed over whether systems are oriented simply towards survival—just maintaining the status quo unless needing to change in order to continue existing—or also are oriented towards achieving ever greater levels of complexity and organization—something which we could call growth. Of course, becoming organized at higher levels of complexity has great survival value, but the question is really whether doing so comes from an inherent impulse within the system or only from environmental pressure. If left on its own, will a system naturally grow, or will it stay the same? Just what is included in the basic purpose of a system...survival only, or also growth?

According to its proponents, part of the intoxicating attraction of systems theory is that it offers us principles which refer to all systems, regardless of type or size. What economy! With just one set of principles, we can understand so many things. The verdict is still out on this claim, however.

Whether *all* systems are oriented merely towards survival, or also towards growth, I do not know. But to this point in time my learning indicates that the human personality system seems to include a strong growth orientation. Given the opportunity, some part of us seems to want to adjust to internal and external changes in such a way that our personality systems become more complex and more highly organized. We tend to aspire to growth, given the chance. Learning to create the chance is what this book is about.

Systemic Adjustments: Maintenance

In order to make progress on this objective, we need to explore what has been learned about the ways in which systems adjust to internal and external changes. Two main types of responses can be identified. They have particular utility for us because they relate directly to the important distinction between *simple change* and *growth* which we made in the last chapter.

First, we will take up a type of adjustment called *self-regulation*. When a system encounters change in its environment or its own parts, it can simply process those changes in order to *maintain* itself. In this case, parts may change, and the environment may change; however, the essential nature of the system's wholeness—the ordered pattern of interrelationship among its parts—remains unchanged.

For example, when a family moves to a new city, its environment may change drastically. New jobs, new schools, a new neighborhood—the environment presents many new elements to which to adapt. The family has certain patterns of interrelationship among its members which somehow define its wholeness and give it an identity. The family as a system processes its new inputs through the function of these existing patterns of internal order. The self-regulatory objective of the family is to retain its identity and internal order while surviving its adjustments to the new environment.

Organizations also provide good examples. Take a college, for instance. The specific individuals which occupy the various roles within a college—its students, faculty, staff, and administrators—change frequently. Also, the social environments in which the college exists—local, state, national, and global—fluctuate continually. Despite all of this internal and external change, however, most colleges retain a clear and seemingly constant identity. Built into their systems are ways to regulate affairs such that the essential organization of the college remains intact.

Individual personalities are also systems which can regulate themselves. As our bodies age, our roles change, our minds acquire knowledge, we have a good deal of internal change to which to adjust. Also, we pass through many social environments in a lifetime, and each context tends to press for adaptation on our part. Built into a personality system is the capacity to make adjustments such that the overall identity remains unchanged. When one part changes—either because of internal or external pressure—other parts adjust; but the overall pattern of relationships among the parts may remain essentially the same.

Systemic Adjustments: Transformation

Change in systems can be seen to exist on two levels: change in *parts,* and change in the *relationship* of the parts. The first kind of adjustment involves *self-regulation.* The second kind of adjustment—which we will take up now—involves what can be called *self-reorganization.*

For example, say that the father in a family, who had fulfilled a "bread-winner" role, stayed home and took care of the children, while the mother, who had been a "housewife," pursued her career and supported the family financially. Not only did two members of the family change, but the nature of their relationship may have changed, perhaps dramatically. In addition, the relationship between each parent and their children probably changed. Because of these adjustments, not just in the individual members of the family, but in the fundamental pattern of interrelationship among the members, the family can be seen to have developed a new type of organization. The way in which the family processes internal and external changes is fundamentally different. It has a new identity, a new order; it is a new whole.

For another example, let's look at a college again. Say that the college's student population changed from being dominated by traditional-age students (18 to 22 years old) to having a predominance of adult students. Not only would the curriculum have to change, but also the way in which that curriculum was delivered to the students. Student services also would have to change substantially. This actually happened at Marylhurst College, where I work. Founded in 1893, as a traditional, four-year, Catholic college for young women, Marylhurst began to encounter empty dorms and an increasing commuter population of adult students in the 1960's. After careful study, the old college was closed in 1974, in order to be reincarnated immediately as Marylhurst College for Lifelong Learning, an educational center which catered to the adult learner. In response to a changing environment, the college reorganized itself to become a new entity, a new whole which not only had new parts but also fundamentally new relationships among its parts.

Personality systems also can manifest a basic reorganization. For example, if a person's self-concept were to change substantially, a profound ripple effect throughout the whole personality would probably result. All we need to do is to think back to the formation of our initial adult identities for a clear image of how this process works. For instance, our impulses still operated, but with a new self-concept—that of an adult rather than a child—these impulses took up a new kind of relationship with our will. This fundamental realignment of relationships can occur extensively in a personality system with the change of such an important element as the self-concept, and the personality can be reorganized to become a new whole.

Systemic Adjustments:
Simple Change vs. Growth

To repeat, a system adjusts itself to internal and external change in one of two ways. It can regulate itself in order to maintain its same basic structure, or it can reorganize itself in order to become a whole new structure. The first kind of adjustment relates to what we described as *simple change* in the last chapter: change but—at a higher level—no change. The second adjustment relates more directly to our initial description of *growth*. Of course, not all reorganization is necessarily growth, and we will discuss just which kind is, and which kind is not, in Chapter 5.

We may have a tendency to place value judgments on these two kinds of adjustments. For example, we may tend to see reorganization as better than maintenance. However, each type of adjustment can be seen to have its place. If our personalities are quite functional and satisfying ("I'm just fine, thank you!"), then reorganization may not be an appropriate gamble.

Some risks always exist in reconstituting something or someone, and this fact may explain why systems often show resistance to reorganization. Maintenance-regulation seems to be the initial response. Reorganization follows the failure of maintenance-regulation to provide an appropriate adjustment.

Incidentally, this pattern—maintenance-regulation first, reorganization second—may reveal why people are often ambivalent about growth. Risk is inherent in the kind of reorganization which characterizes growth. Our personalities (as systems) tend to resist reorganization unless maintenance-regulation is not working. However, a human personality may be a special kind of system because embedded in it seems to be a powerful element which wars against this resistance and urges the personality on to growth. When the person is not threatened, the maintenance forces often have the upper hand. However, when the person is threatened, and maintenance is not working, growth's reorganization forces are joined by simple survival urges, and reorganization gains the crucial advantage.

This pattern may be one of the reasons why growth is often associated with trauma. The person frequently maintains the status quo until its dysfunction becomes clear and things start to fall apart. In these situations, the person usually feels uncertain as to whether the outcome will be a new person, or no person at all. We say that we are "falling apart" because the phrase characterizes what it feels like when our personalities seem to be staggering along a thin line separating transformation from disintegration.

However, growth need not be associated with trauma. We need to learn to understand the objective of our natural resistance to reorganization—our own survival. We also need to learn how to promote and bolster the growth motivation within us so that it doesn't need to be joined by a survival scare in order to prevail over our maintenance motivation. We need to learn how to work out win-win solutions for these two urges within us. From this learning, growth can become a *proactive* endeavor—something which *we plan and manage*—rather than a *reactive* event— something which willy-nilly *happens to us.* Parts II and III will provide concrete strategies for creating these win-win solutions.

Hierarchies of Interrelated Systems

Before closing this chapter, we should discuss one more property of systems which is particularly germane to our interest in human development. Recall that systems can be of any size: atoms are systems, and the universe is a system; an attitude is a system, and the whole personality is a system. Large or small, they are all systems. What is evident from these examples is that most *wholes* (most systems) are also *parts* of larger wholes. A system can be a whole and a part *simultaneously.* The important point here is that systems tend to be organized into hierarchies with the smallest, least-extensive systems on the bottom and the largest, most-extensive ones on the top.

For example, each employee in an organization is a personality system. Each office of which the employee is a part is also a system, just as is each division of which each office is a part, and so on, all the way up to the system of the overall organization, and beyond.

Or, consider that each thing that we know is a system. Each of these knowledge "units" are parts of our overall cognitive system. Our cognitive system is a part of our overall personality system. Notice the levels, or orders, or generality.

Utility of the Hierarchy Concept

Why is knowing this hierarchal property of systems useful for us? At least three reasons exist.

First, this knowledge encourages us to use our systems' insights for any scale of growth projects—large or small. Whether we are trying to become a whole new person, or we are simply trying to improve our tennis game, the systems perspective is equally useful. Each part of ourselves can be seen as a system in itself and, therefore, as a suitable object for our principles of systemic change.

Second, being aware of the hierarchical property of systems sensitizes us to the possibility of ripple effects from any particular change. For example, if the personality of one member of a family changes, the whole family system may ultimately be changed in a radical way, or hardly at all, depending on the interaction of the other family members with the person who changes. Or, using a previous example, changing the cognitive system which constitutes our self-concept may eventually change our whole personality system. Changing a part may eventually result in changing the whole, and we need to be aware of this possibility.

Finally, with this sensitivity to the interrelationship of levels, we can become increasingly sophisticated about which parts exert the most influence on the nature of the overall whole. We can use this knowledge of specific ripple effects in service of our particular growth objectives. For example, an important facet of the art of cognitive therapy is knowing which cognitive systems have the most far-reaching impact on the overall personality. Not all of our beliefs are equally potent in terms of their influence on our essential character, and knowing which ones really count can lead to substantial growth.

The properties which have been discussed in this chapter represent some of the fundamental features of systems. Although on some mornings we may feel like heaps, each of us is really a whole, and these properties of systems apply to us, as well as to our families, organizations, societies, planet, and universe. As we will see later, these principles, and the general perspective of which they are a part, will be very handy as we try to discern just what growth is, and how to help it to happen.

CHAPTER **4**

PEOPLE AS CONTENT AND PROCESS

Some thirty inches from my nose
The frontier of my Person goes
And all the untilled air between
Is private *pagus* or demesne.
Stranger, unless with bedroom eyes
I beckon you to fraternize
Beware of rudely crossing it:
I have no gun, but I can spit.

W. H. Auden,
"Prologue: The Birth of Architecture" (1965, p. 4)

I hate to admit it, but I really don't know how my car works. When I raise the hood, the engine looks like a miniature jungle to me. Tubes and wires and metal contraptions seem to grow right before my very eyes in a confusion of mechanical verdure. Whenever I foolishly venture into my car's heart of darkness, I swear that wild animals spring from the shadows and claw my knuckles and bite my fingers. My safari jacket is quickly devoured, and I lose my pithe helmet. Frantic in this hostile forest, I look for safe escape as oil and gasoline begin to rain down on my head. Tortuous hours later, I emerge from the perilous jungle, tattered of mind and body, smudged of face and persona, but grateful that my wounded fingers still have the strength to stagger through the yellow pages in search of a good mechanic.

I can't work on my car very well because I don't know how it works. I don't know all of the parts and how they fit together. So, when my car isn't running well, I hire a specialist to fix it.

In this book, we are interested in people not cars. But the same principle applies: working on something is difficult when you lack a framework for it. Our objective is to learn to prosper as much as possible without calling in a specialist.

So, in this chapter, as a final step before exploring a definition of development, we need to sketch out a simple framework for thinking about that which we are trying to develop: ourselves. Just what are the basic elements of the person as defined by Auden's "frontier"?

MIND/BODY SYSTEM

To keep things succinct, we will say that the person is a *mind/body system* with interrelated *formal* and *functional* properties. A proverb teaches that one picture speaks a thousand words, so perhaps the following figure will help to communicate the connections among these four elements:

	Forms	**Functions**
Mind		
Body		

Schematic for connections among four components: mind and body systems (person) with interrelated formal and functional properties.

Picture or no, a little explanation of this framework is in order. Let's begin with the mind, since this book clearly emphasizes that aspect of the person.

FORMAL PROPERTIES OF THE MIND

Just what do we mean by the formal and functional properties of the mind? First, we will take up mental forms, or the content, of our minds.

Our Mental Forms: Our Realities

Each of us lives in a world which is an important way we ourselves construct. The theory of "Immaculate Perception" has long since bitten the dust. Given the same stimulus object, all people simply do not perceive the same thing. This fact is perhaps no more dramatically encountered than when we interact with someome from another culture. The anthropologist Colin Turnbull illustrated this point humorously and poignantly when he described the reactions of Kenge, his Pygmy companion, as they left the familiar rain forest and Kenge encountered the Central African mountains and plains for the first time. Like most forest people, Kenge had never experienced being able to see great distances, and so his perceptions were very different from those of Turnbull:

> When Kenge topped the rise, he stopped dead.... Down below us, on the far side of the hill, stretched mile after mile of rolling grassland, a lush, fresh green, with an occasional shrub or tree standing out like a sentinel into a sky that had suddenly become brilliantly clear.... It was like nothing Kenge had ever seen before...
>
> Then he saw the buffalo, still grazing lazily several miles away, far down below. He turned to me and said, "What insects are those?"...
>
> When I told Kenge that the insects were buffalo, he roared with laughter and told me not to tell such stupid lies....
>
> The road led on down to within about half a mile of where the herd was grazing, and as we got closer, the "insects" must have seemed to get bigger and bigger. Kenge, who was now sitting on the outside, kept his face glued to the window, which nothing would make him lower. I even had to raise mine to keep him happy. I was never able to discover just what he thought was happening—whether he thought the insects were changing into buffalo, or that they were miniature buffalo growing rapidly as we approached. His only comment was that they were not real buffalo, and he was not going to get out of the car until we left the park. (Turnbull, 1961, pp. 251-253)

This example may seem exotic, but many of us react as Kenge did when we encounter something from outside of our known worlds. We have our own ideas of how things are in the universe, and if something does not conform with these ideas, it falls into that often disturbing category of being "unreal." Notice that Kenge not only declared that the animals were not real buffalo but also decided to stay in the safety of the car, a known environment, until he left that strange place. How many times have we done something like that before?

Beliefs

These ideas we have of *how things are* comprise our system of *beliefs*. We glorify the beliefs in which we feel most certain by calling them facts. But in the final analysis, facts are beliefs just the same. In terms of our framework, our beliefs are a major type of *mental form*, a major category of the *contents* of our minds. So, they represent an important *formal* property of the mind.

Attitudes

However, we do not feel equally positive or negative about the various parts of the world which we construct in our belief system. We have *attitudes* towards things. We like some ideas, and dislike others; we adore some people, and abhor others. Even if we see the same thing which other people see, we may feel differently about it than they do. In other words, our beliefs can be charged with emotional valences and consequently have behavioral tendencies associated with them.

For instance, in contrasting the management practices in Japan with those in the United States, Richard Pascale and Anthony Athos pointed out significant differences in the two cultures' attitude towards ambiguity. When a Japanese manager and an American manager encounter a situation which both would agree is ambiguous, each tends to respond in a different way.

> In the United States...when a situation is "ambiguous," the implication is that it is incomplete, unstable, and needs clearing up. In Japan, in contrast, ambiguity is seen as having both desirable and undesirable aspects.... More ambiguity, uncertainty, and imperfection in organizations is acceptable to [the Japanese] than to [the Americans] as an immutable fact of life, what philosophers in the West have called "existential givens." By this they mean that such conditions just *are*.... Regarding them as *enemies* gets our adrenaline pumping for a hopeless battle. Regarding them as conditions to be reduced or lived with, as appropriate to the situation, makes more sense. (Pascale & Athos, 1981, p. 141).

Pascale and Athos then went on to illustrate how the Japanese attitude toward ambiguity is interrelated with the Japanese language (a collection of mental forms for the culture).

The Japanese embrace an idea of the world that says, although there is "nothing" there is still something. Consider this analogy: in English we often refer to an empty space as, for example, "the space between the chair and the table." In the Japanese equivalent, the space isn't "empty"; it's "full of nothing." The illustration makes this point: Westerners speak of what is unknown primarily in reference to what is known (i.e., of the space between the chair and the table); the Japanese view of "nothing" illustrates that dignity can be given to emptiness in its own right. One finds symbols of this in a Zen garden, where a few large rocks stand alone in a sea of raked pebbles. Westerners see the rocks; the Japanese are trained to pay attention to the space around them. (Pascale & Athos, 1981, p. 142)

Values

These illustrations not only point out the interrelationship between our beliefs and attitudes (how we think things are, and how we feel about those things), but also, they suggest a third important element of the mind's formal properties—*values* (how we think things *should* be). For example, when the American manager encounters an ambiguous situation in the organization, he/she feels that things *ought* to be cleared up. Uncertainty is bad; certainty is good. In the American value system, the good manager *should* do something to achieve clarity. When a Japanese manager runs into a similar situation, different value filters (different mental forms) prescribe different behavior. In the Japanese value system, the good manager *should* be able to function effectively and comfortably with ambiguity, since ambiguity is seen to be an ever present companion in life.

We do not need to go as far away as Japan, however, in order to find differences between people which illustrate what values are. For example, take a couple in which the man holds the value that people should not "dump" their feelings on others, while the woman feels that people should share their feelings with their partners as a manifestation of intimacy. Each partner does what he/she thinks should be done, as they slowly drive each other crazy.

These, then, are three basic concepts regarding our *mental forms: beliefs* (what we think is real and true), *attitudes* (how we feel about the various parts of our realities and truths), and *values* (what we think should be real and true). So much for some of important formal properties of the mind, now we turn our attention to its functional properties.

FUNCTIONAL PROPERTIES OF THE MIND

Functional properties involve the mind in action. Whereas the formal properties comprise the world which each of us constructs (the *content* of our minds), the functional properties refer to the ways in which we construct that world and relate to it. Functional properties involve the mind as a *process*, the mind as a *verb*.

Rather than thoughts (mental forms), functional characteristics involve thinking. Rather than feelings, the mind's functions involve feeling. Rather than perceptions, perceiving. Rather than values, valuing. And so on. With functional properties, we refer to the mind as process rather than content.

CONTRASTING THE MIND'S FORMAL
AND FUNCTIONAL PROPERTIES

George Herbert Mead has provided a good example of the difference between the formal and functional properties of the mind with his concepts of the "me" and the "I" (Mead, 1962). In Mead's scheme, the "me" translates into what we would call our self-concept. It involves the me which we think ourselves to be. The "I," on the other hand, is that which does the thinking, that which does the conceptualizing of the self, that which forms the image of the "me."

Experiencing the difference between the "I" and the"me" is easy enough. Try for a moment to sit perfectly still and concentrate on yourself. Focus on your breathing to get started. In and out...relax... Next, expand your awareness to your whole being. Think about who you are. This is the "me." Then, quickly shift to thinking about that which is thinking about who you are. This is the "I." Jump up to another level: think about that which is thinking about who you are. This is the "I" again.

We realize from these playful gymnastics that a part of us is pure process—the "I." As soo as it becomes the object of our attention, it is no longer the "I"; it becomes the "me." The "I" is that to which we are referring when we speak of the functional properties of the mind.

INTERRELATIONSHIP OF FORMAL
AND FUNCTIONAL PROPERTIES

The formal and functional properties of the mind and body are interrelated, which is importance to remember as we go about our developmental endeavors.

The Mind

For examples of this interrelationship of mental forms and functions, we need only recall those times when we wanted to improve our abilities to think, feel, and act in a certain way (a developmental project which relates to our mind's functional abilities). To make this improvement, we may had to change our self-concept or our conceptualizations of certain situations (mental forms).

Trying to control anger provides a good example. Sometimes we carry in our minds some unreasonable expectations—some might say utopian visions—of how people should act. As a result, everyday life becomes one disappointment and frustrations after another. We see the problem as being people acting irresponsibly, and it can infuriate us. When we come to realize that the larger problem may be the way in which we are conceptualizing the problem, we may make a breakthrough on controlling our anger. Incidentally, Watzlawick, Weakland, and Fisch have contributed a great deal to our understanding of meta-problems such as this "Utopia Syndrome" in their book, *Change: Principles of Problem Formation and Problem Resolution* (1974). In our example, perhaps the difficulty is not that people are so irresponsible but rather that our expectations are so unreasonable. Our plight may be that too often we perceive a problem with other people's behavior when no reasonable problem exists. With a change in our expectations (our mental forms), reducing our outrage (a mental function) becomes much easier.

Or here's an example of the reverse—of how changes in one of our mental functions (processes) can affect our mental forms (contents). Empathy is a skill which facilitates communication immensely, and many people—whether for personal or professional reasons—engage in training to improve their empathic perception. Empathy means experiencing the other person's thoughts, feelings, and bodily states as if we were actually that other person (Wispé, 1968). To perform this act, we must suspend our own frame of reference for a moment and imagine ourselves to be the other person. The result of this process can be that we have an intimate experience of another reality, a world which is sometimes quite exotic to our own. As we incorporate this experience into our own perspective, we may see a real change in our own beliefs, attitudes, and values—that is, in our mind's formal properties. Improving our empathic skills in our intimate relationships provides a good example of this phenomenon. As people become more empathic with their partners, or with people in general, they frequently find that their view of the world is expanded and enriched in a desirable way. From an improvement of the mind's functional properties (processes) can come an embellishment of the mind's formal properties (contents).

The point here is that the formal and functional properties of the mind interrelate significantly. Making the distinction between formal and functional properties is useful in our developmental projects because it helps us to pinpoint our primary objectives. Do we want to work on our thoughts, or on our thinking? However, we always must remember that whether we wish to focus on developing content or process we will want to use both the formal and functional elements of the mind in order to achieve the desired outcome.

The Body

Now, we will add a brief word about the body. The formal and functional properties of the body are much more obvious than those of the mind. The mind's forms involve intangible thoughts and feelings, and the mind's functions refer to the elusive "I." However, the body's formal and functional properties—its contents and processes—designate elements of the person which have clear physical dimensions. By formal properties of the body, we simply mean bones, muscles, organs, neurons, and such. By functional properties, we mean the way in which these various physical parts of the body work. Anatomy and physiology are the two branches of biology which study each of these aspects of the human body—anatomy having to do with bodily forms (contents), and physiology with bodily functions (processes). A biology lesson would stray from the primary interests of this book, but the important interrelationship of these two aspects of the human body is worth noting. Quite simply, you can't go all day full tilt if you're out of shape.

Mind and Body

We need to remember in creating this conceptual framework— in this taking apart of the person—that the various elements of the framework all go together to form a single system. The mind and the body—each with its formal functional properties—interrelate to constitute a whole: the person. Some examples of the inter- relationship of mind and body might be useful at this point.

I have a friend who gets sick when she visits her family without her husband. Her parents and her sister's family are all decent people, but a great deal of unfinished business lingers between herself and her mother, father, and sister. The stress of these longstanding psychological conflicts takes a toll on her body. She tends to become run down and consequently to become highly vulnerable to whatever illness is going around at the time. However, when her partner is with her to help her to process interactions with her family, she fares much better. Psychological stress provides many excellent examples of the effect which mental states can have on the body.

Of course, bodily states also can affect the mind. For example, take exercise. During particular types of vigorous physical activity, the body can produce morphine-like substances called endor- phins. The result of this bodily production can be a very pleasant state of mind, a natural "high."

We could continue at length about the interconnectedness of mind and body. Based on a depending understanding of this profound relationship between psyche and soma, mental health professionals are are becoming increasingly concerned with their clients' nutrition, exercise patterns, genetic background, and so forth, just as medical doctors are becoming increasingly sensitive to the psycho-social characteristics of their patients and their patients' environments. As growth-agents, we would do well to be aware of this interconnectedness as well.

The person is a system with mental and physical parts. As systems, each of us manifests all of the general characteristics of systems which were explained in the preceding chapter: wholeness, self-regulation, self-reorganization, and interconnected hierarchies of sub-systems.

With the framework of the person which has been developed in this chapter, and with these systems' principles, we begin to acquire the basic perspectival tools of the effective growth-agent. We now have a coherent set of general categories in order to identify the parts of ourselves on which we wish to focus our particular developmental projects. We have a better understanding of how "secondary" elements which are peripheral to our developmental focus may affect, and be affected by, the outcomes of our developmental projects. We have the conceptual frameworks in order to begin to think about which of our various parts are most influential in changing our whole.

The basic tool which we still lack is a clear and broadly applicable definition of development. Just what does it mean to grow, either in our parts or in our whole? A definition of development is the final piece necessary to enable us to formulate effective objectives in our specific growth endeavors. For what are we aiming? The next chapter provides us with an answer to this question.

CHAPTER 5

A DEFINITION OF DEVELOPMENT

A mischievous child accidentally set fire to a house with a pig inside, and the villagers poking around in the embers discovered a new delicacy. This eventually led to a rash of house fires. The moral of the story is: when you do not understand how the pig gets cooked, you have to burn a whole house down every time you want a roast-pig dinner.

Rosabeth Moss Kanter,
Change Masters (1983, p. 302)

I hate to think of the number of times I have burned down my whole house in order to obtain the delicacy of development. Leaving relationships, leaving jobs, dropping projects, moving—these things I have done because I thought that dramatic, house-fire change was necessary to produce growth. Never mind that I was often too traumatized from my losses to enjoy the roast pork, or that sometimes I couldn't find the prize among the ashes. Never mind that I even became phobic about pork, and tried my best to do without it. "Roast pork! Anything but roast pork!" Conflagration and growth, they just seemed to go together.

This unfortunate association resulted from my ignorance about the nature of development, and how it is produced. I simply did not know what I was doing. My objectives were ambiguous. My strategies were bizarre. My resources were unrecognized or mishandled. And since I did not have a clear idea of what I was trying to accomplish, I rarely had a firm sense that I had accomplished anything, except of course burning down my house.

What I really needed was a deeper understanding of growth. What I needed was a good theory (a shorthand for this deeper understanding) which I could carry around in my head and apply to new situations. With this theory, I could generate insightful objectives, effective strategies, good resources, and a meaningful basis for evaluating and correcting my growth endeavors. Without a good theory, I would remain in the realm of superstitious trial and error.

With the sincerest good will, I hope that you have experienced similar follies, for as Alfred, Lord Tennyson reminded us (1899c, p. 140):

> And others' follies teach us not,
>   Nor much their wisdom teaches;
> And most of sterling worth is what
>   Our own experience preaches.

I'm betting that you have your own history of pyromania and will be ready for some helpful theory.

In this chapter, we will explore a simple, transportable definition of development. This definition will build on our previous discussions regarding the difference between simple change and growth, the basic principles of systems, and a framework for the nature of the person. The definition is grounded in common human events, and as usual, we will develop it by considering situations which many of us have experienced. The definition will simply put into a few words what many of us may already know at some tacit level.

RECALLING THE EXPERIENCE OF GROWTH

Let's begin by referring to the "home movies" from Chapter 2. Recall once again that growth experience which you chose to re-live in the visualization exercise, that experience in which you felt that you really grew, whether in a specific part of your personal or professional life, or in an overall way as a whole person. Remember the events of this transition. What were your thoughts, feelings, and actions as you participated in these events? How about the thoughts, feelings, and actions of those around you? How did you change? How did your relationships change? If you recorded some highlights after our exercise, review those notes now.

Also, recall the change-but-no-change episode which you chose to re-experience, the time during which you went through a dramatic change but without growth. Again, remember the events, your inner states, your outer behavior, the nature of the changes. Review your notes if you have them.

As examples of what other people have said when asked to reflect on these two kinds of experiences, you read a number of personal stories in Chapter 2. Remember the examples of growth experiences which were developed: the middle-age man who had needed to adjust to his wife's spectacular re-entry into professional life in contrast to his own stagnation, the middle-age woman who took up college and career in response to her husband's affair, and the professor who learned to be a manager as a result of his promotion to departmental chairperson. Also, recall the change-but-no-growth examples: the woman whose family's upwardly mobile re-location in a new city only underscored how miserable she was, the person who changed companies but not jobs, and the man who repeatedly changed partners but never the pattern of his intimate relationships.

When we contrast these two types of experiences—growth and simple change—a general principle emerges: *growth involves some kind of transformation of the self.* Whether we are looking at our own experiences or those of other people, whether the experiences relate to our whole selves or to some specific part of us, whether they be in the personal or professional domains of our lives, growth involves transformation. *Growth is the birth of something new in us.*

ABSTRACTING A DEFINITION OF GROWTH

With this realization as background, we are now ready to venture into a general definition of development-as-growth (if interested in selections of the psychological theory which help to inform this definition, see Gilligan, 1982; Kegan, 1982; Kohlberg, 1969, 1973; Kohlberg, Levine, & Hewer, 1983; Loevinger & Blasi, 1976; Perry, 1970; Piaget & Inhelder, 1969; Sanford, 1966; and Werner, 1948):

Growth = Addition + Transformative Integration

With growth, we *add* something new to ourselves—to our minds or our bodies, to our content or our processes. The addition may be a new bit of knowledge, or a new mental skill. The addition may be more inches to our height if we are young, or a new physical ability. However, growth is not just a *quantitative* change—more of something, more knowledge, more cells. Growth also has an essential *qualitative* dimension. The new thing must be *integrated* into what we already are if it is truly to become part of us. It must become integrated into the whole—the system—which you and I call me. If with this integration, a *transformation* of the system, or its sub-systems, occurs—large or small—then growth has transpired.

*Growth involves quantitative **and** qualitative changes, but not one without the other.* Remember that we are dynamic, open systems with permeable boundaries, and consequently, that we are constantly processing and incorporating new things which come from our environments and which arise from within us. In Chapter 3, we talked about how systems can maintain their essential character even while adding new elements, that is, of how systems can become quantitatively different *without* becoming qualitatively different. This is *not* growth. This is a case of change-but-no-growth. Also, in Chapter 3, we spoke about how systems can re-organize themselves to change their essential character, that is, of how systems can become quantitatively *and* qualitatively different. This *is* growth.

CONTENT EXAMPLE

At this point, a few concrete illustrations of this definition are probably in order. for these examples, let's focus on the mind—its formal and functional properties, its content and processes—since that is the primary interest of this book. First, we begin with an illustration of content growth.

Expanding Women's Roles

The phenomenon of expanding roles for women can provide a good example of growth of the mind's formal properties. In recent years, an increasing number of women have demanded of men, and of themselves, greater diversity in the number of acceptable roles available to them. Women want to have legitimate access to roles of leadership as well as of nurturance. They want to be able to become doctors as well as nurses, chief executive offices as well as administrative assistants, breadwinners as well as housewives. Sex roles exist most significantly in our minds, and women do not want to be limited by narrow cognitive systems which put them as the power *behind* the throne. Women wan to be able to be *in* the throne if they have the talent, drive, and desire to achieve it. They want the society which our minds create to provide freedom rather than restriction, to be open and dynamic rather than closed and rigid. They want us to develop further our mental images of women.

Application of the Definition

In terms of our definition of development, the challenge of expanding women's sex roles fits perfectly. With this particular transition in the society which our minds hold, we have the *addition* of possible roles for women. Our cognitive system which sets what we think is appropriate for women has parts *added to it.* Women can be career professionals as well as wives. They can buy flowers for men as well as have flowers bought for them by men. They can pursue as well as be pursued. They can be explorers of open spaces as well as tenders of the home-fires. This new mentality does not require that a woman fulfill *all* of these roles— that is, be a "Superwoman." Rather, in our minds, the array of appropriate possibilities from which a woman can choose has new entries added to it.

The description of this new array suggests, however, that with development we have more than simply added new roles for women. Growth is *addition* plus *integration*. Sex role development does not just mean learning to out-macho the machos at the expense of important nurturing qualities. It does not mean just getting a dark suit, a bow blouse, and a "new *femme d affaires* haircut hard as nails" (Hoffman, 1983). We probably all know some very unhappy women who have repressed their nuturing sides in order to compete in the male-dominated professional world. This strategy of *adding* "male" qualities to the self-concept while trying to *subtract* "female" qualities, rather than *integrating* "male" and "female" qualities, can extract a tremendous psychic cost for the individual. While it may provide some professional success, it is *not* development. With development, we add and integrate, not add and subtract. Actually, subtracting the old is impossible under normal circumstances; we simply *repress* the old, which is often a crippling adjustment. Our choice is really only whether we integrate the new with the old, or add the new and repress the old. With repression can come problems. With integration, and the transformation which it provokes, comes development.

Complexity, flexibility, and *stability,* these are the hallmarks of growth (Werner, 1948). And with the *addition* and *transformative integration* of new roles into our image of women, we can see that these qualities are increased in our image, and that mental development has occurred.

Increasing Complexity

With the *addition* of new roles for women, and with the *integration* of these new roles with former roles, we have the kind of *transformation* of our cognitive image of women which qualifies as *mental development.* Our minds' image of women—whether we are men or women—has become more *complex.* The image not only has more parts, but it is organized at a higher level of generalization. It has both greater depth and greater breadth.

Increasing Flexibility

Also, our cognitive image has become more *flexible.* It can account for more situations which we encounter in our everyday living without evoking the "Kenge" response of freezing in the face of the "unreal" buffaloes and declaring them to be bad. With greater complexity, our image becomes better able to flex with our changing realities.

Increasing Stability

Finally, with this addition and transformative integration regarding women's roles, this part of our cognitive system has become more *stable.* Mark Twain is supposed to have said, "It is not so much what people don't know that makes trouble, as what people know that ain't so." Women not only *can* fulfill more roles, they *are* fulfilling more roles. Thinking that they can't "makes trouble" when we encounter the fact that they are. Because our cognitive system has acquired the complexity and flexibility to accomodate our common intra- and inter-personal experiences—because it has a good fit with our complex realities—our image of women becomes less volatile and resists dramatic and dysfunctional swings from one extreme to another in response to the diversity of these experiences. F. Scott Fitzgerald seemed to have had this kind of stability in mind when he wrote, "...the test of a first-rate intelligence is the ability to hold two opposed ideas in the mind at the same time, and still retain the ability to function" (Fitzgerald, 1945, p. 69). This test may also be a good indicator of development—stable integrity which accomodates great diversity.

Ripple Effects

Our minds are systems, and changing one part of them can precipitate changes in other parts. Developing further the number and variety of appropriate roles for women can have a number of ripple effects in our cognitive system.

For example, changing women's roles encourages the further development of men's roles. Increasing the possibilities for women clearly has tended to stimulate an increase in the possible roles for men. The current social environment demands us—men and women alike—to add to our conception of the number of appropriate roles which men can fill, and then to integrate these additions with the kinds of roles which men have filled in the past. The entire discussion of the development of men's roles, including the important caveat about the dangers of representing former roles rather than integrating the new roles with the old ones.

As our conception of women's and men's roles develop and move from different directions toward a complex androgyny, our images of appropriate male/female relationship forms are encouraged to develop. Increasing the number of appropriate possibilities for each partner produces the need to expand our conception of the range of appropriate combinations.

The list of ripple effects could continue. For example, adding and integrating new forms of male/female relationships in turn precipitates the development of our images of important social institutions such as marriage, family and the workplace.

However, I think that you probably get the point. If we transform one important element of our overall cognitive system—in this case, our conception of appropriate roles for women—we may also trigger the development of more inclusive, cognitive subsystems of which that element is a part. As the effects ripple out, we can see that by developing our conception of women, we also may end up developing our conception of the whole society. This case illustrates well, with regard to the content of our minds, the kind of systemic dynamics which are encompassed by our definition of development.

PROCESS EXAMPLE

For a second illustration of our definition of development, we will turn from the formal properties of the mind—its contents—in order to emphasize its functional properties—its processes. The process on which we will focus will be our ability to *learn*, an ability which we will see throughout this book not only can be an object of our development but also is essential to the developmental process itself.

Learning

First, we need to say a word about what learning is. David Kolb provides us with a very useful model for thinking about this mental process (Kolb, 1984). Since we will be referring to his framework at various points in the remainder of the book, we need to spend a little time coming to terms with it. In his "experiential learning model," Kolb describes the person's learning process in terms of two dimensions: a dimension in which we *grasp* the learning either *concretely* or *abstractly*, and a dimension in which we *transform* the learning in order to make it our own either *reflectively* or *actively*. Put simple, he says that a complete learning cycle involves the person having *concrete experiences*, *reflecting* on these experiences, formulating *abstract generalizations* about them, and *experimenting* to explore the validity and implications of the generalizations. A simple diagram helps to portray the relationship of these operations (after Kolb, 1984):

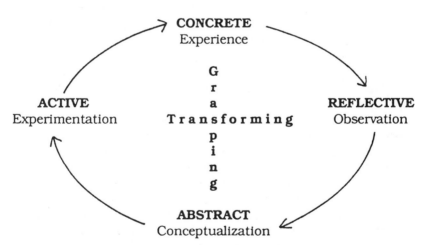

Whether we are in the classroom or in the street, at home or at the office, whether we are working with colleagues or computers, with relatives or plumbing, we each use all four of these skills in order to make sense of our worlds, that is, in order to learn. Each of these mental processes can be seen as a separate skill, but they all go together to form the larger skill of learning.

Given that we each use all four of these skills, however, many of us prefer some parts of the learning cycle over others. For example, some us may love to dive into things with nothing in particular in mind, just to see what happens (*concrete experience*). Others may thoroughly enjoy ruminating on experiences (*reflective observation*), exploring all of the details of what was going on—what the various participants did and when, what they were thinking and feeling, what they were trying to do—teasing out all of the specific implications of what has transpired. Some of us may prefer forming ideas based on these experiences and ruminations (*abstract conceptualization*)—identifying the major variables which were involved and the relationships among these variables in order to forge some general principles or hypotheses out of the raw experience. Others of us may feel most at home when the time comes to try out these ideas (*active experimentation*), when the time comes to get "out there" and do something, but with a purpose, with a plan, with something in mind which may make things easier and better, something which needs testing. In other words, some of us like to be *explorers;* some like to be *meditators;* some like to be *philosophers;* and some like to be *scientists.* Some people prefer the *concrete* over the *abstract;* while for others, the reverse is true. And some people prefer *reflection* over *action;* while for others, vice versa.

Out of these preferences for various parts of the learning cycle—various sub-skills within the larger skill of learning—comes our particular "learning style." Different learning styles are neither *good* nor *bad;* they are just *different.* People with contrasting learning styles often think that each other (or themselves) are "stupid" or "strange." Many relationship problems at home or at the office can be nipped in the bud if we remain sensitive to the simple fact that people process the world differently...not just that we come up with different answers to the meaning of experience, but that we actually go about making meaning in different ways.

Kolb also says that learning styles can develop throughout our lives, and he delineates three developmental stages. Typcially, we begin by acquiring an awareness of our preferred learning style as a part of fundamental identity formation culminating late in adolescence. Social forces involved in our establishing our adult life then encourage specialization within this learning style. Finally, often around midlife, we hear our "hidden voices" and feel the urge to improve the nondominant aspects of our learning cycle.

Application of the Definition

Raising the issue of learning style development brings us back to our definition of development-as-growth. The way in which our learning abilities can develop throughout our lives illustrates our definition beautifully. As we *add* new skills of concrete experience, reflective observation, abstract conceptualization, or active experimentation, and as we *integrate* these additions with our previous skills, our overall learning ability is *transformed* in a positive way.

For example, take concrete experience—the entry point of information into our learning cycle. Let's say that our typical way of interacting with our worlds is one of detachment—that we tend to stay within our own frame of reference and look out at events rather than to immerse ourselves in other peoples' frames and be in the moment of events. Let's say that our tendency is to be *spectators* rather than *participants* (incidentally, Maslow makes this distinction nicely in his book, *The Psychology of Science*, 1966). Perhaps we come to realize that although being a spectator has some advantages, being able to be a participant is also useful. After all, our experiential modes are what determine the kind of material on which we have to reflect, about which we have to generalize, and with which we have to shape our experiments. We may come to see that being able to use a variety of experiential modes in order to collect a diverse array of material is vitally important to our meaning-making processes. We also may come to understand that detaching ourselves from our worlds can lead us to feel alienated and lonely, while in contrast, participating more fully in experience can help us to feel more connected and alive. Martin Buber had a great deal to say about the positive psychological and spiritual impacts of this kind of connectedness in his little classic, *I and Thou* (1970).

The primary tool of the participant is empathy, and as a part of our development in the skill area of concrete experience, let's say that we attempt to become more empathic. Remember that empathy is the ability to experience the world as other people do—the ability to experience other peoples' thoughts, feelings, and even bodily states (Wispé, 1968). Empathy is a skill which can be learned and improved. In broad terms, empathy includes the subskills of being able to suspend our own frame of reference, guide our imagination into the other person's experience, regain ourselves, and incorporate our empathic perceptions into our perspective (Bennett, 1979; Katz, 1963).

In terms of our definition of development, we can see that as we *add* to our techniques of suspending and regaining the self, as well as add to our skills of guided imagination and the incorporation of our imaginings into our own perspective, *and* as we *integrate* these new skills with our existing skills in these areas, we *transform* our empathic abilities. Furthermore, we can see that as we develop our empathy, we *add* to our skills in the more general skill area of concrete experience. As we *integrate* our new skills in concrete experience with our existing skills in the other areas of the learning cycle—reflective observation, abstract conceptualization, and active experimentation—our overall learning skill is *transformed* to become more complex, flexible, and stable. In other words, our ability to learn grows. Such is growth's potential ripple effect through the hierarchy of our various systems.

USEFULNESS OF THE DEFINITION

These examples point out several interesting features of this definition of development.

Fits Any Scale

First, the examples show that the definition can be applied to any *scale* of a person. Whether we focus on our ability to suspend our own frame of reference, or more generally, on our ability to empathize with others, or still more generally, on our ability to learn, or even more generally, on our overall ability to function productively in our worlds—whatever the scale of our focus, large or small, a part of ourselves or our whole selves—we are still dealing with *addition* and *transformative integration* when we speak of growth.

Fits Any Aspect

Second, these examples suggest that our definition of growth applies equally well to all parts of the person—not to just any *scale* of part but also to any *type* of part. Whether we are interested in developing our sex role constructs or our learning abilities—whether we are concentrating on the formal or functional properties of our minds or our bodies—we are still concerned with *adding* new things, *integrating* the new with the old, and thereby *transforming* the object of our development to become more complex, flexible, and stable. We can see that with this definition, we have a "tube-socks" theory of development—one size fits all.

Explains the Past

The benefit of the tube sock is that it fits just about any size or type of foot. Similarly, the benefit of this definition of development is that it fits just about any person or situation. Most of us know what it feels like to have experienced growth—the "ah-hah," "quantum leap," "watershed," "new plateau," or "breakthrough" experience. However, few of us can explain just exactly what has happened, or how. This definition gives us a framework for re-examining our past growth experiences—and those of others—in order to learn from them. What were the *additions* which took place? Which formal or functional properties were involved? What were the various *integrations* which occurred? What conditions promoted these new additions and syntheses? How were we *transformed* as a result? What was the extent of the transformation? What were its consequences? Using this framework to ask good questions, and to answer them, helps us to take advantage of one of our most valuable assets—our own experience.

Plans the Future

This definition is not only useful in looking at the *past*, however. It is also very handy in *planning for the future.* The definition can help us to become more *proactive* with regard to growth—something which is very important as you will recall from our discussion in Chapter 1. Rather than asking, "What *were* the additions which took place?" we ask, "What *will be* the additions which *will* take place?" ...and so on with all of the questions listed above. Just as our framework can help us to understand what *has happened* in our growth experiences, it can also lead us to see what *will need to happen* if growth is to occur in some future experience. This helps us to plan more wisely than we can without a good theory. Our objectives become more specific, realistic, and well-targeted. Our resources and strategies emerge more readily. And finally, evaluating our growth projects effectively and making critical adjustments becomes a much simpler task. Knowing just what we are trying to do makes planning for how to do it much easier. And planning wisely often makes all the difference in the world as to whether or not our wish comes true.

Enhances the Present

Of course, understanding our *past* experiences and planning for *future* experiences are activities which occur in our *present* experience, and which enhance its quality. That's really what this book is all about: enriching the quality of our moment to moment existence. With our framework, we can better know what is happening to us at the moment, and with it, we can better connect that moment with past and future moments so as to gain more influence over the nature of our present experience. With this framework we not only can better "unstick" ourselves, but we also get "stuck" less often.

So, we leave this chapter with that for which we set out: a useful and broadly applicable definition of development. We now have a better idea of what the "it" is which we pursue in our growth projects. However, one more item is essential to a general discussion of development: its phases. Just what are the patterns of transition associated with growth? What are these patterns' key elements, sequences, and timing? We will take up these important questions in our next chapter.

CHAPTER **6**

DEVELOPMENTAL PHASES

> No one discovers a new world without
> forsaking an old one; and no one
> discovers a new world who exacts
> guarantee in advance for what it shall
> be, or who puts the act of discovery
> under bonds with respect to what the new
> world shall do to him when it comes.
>
> John Dewey, *Experience and Nature*
> (1958, p. 246)

Growth involves discovering a new world. As we add and integrate parts within ourselves, we and our worlds are transformed. Granted, sometimes the transformation is small and doesn't qualify as a whole world of change. But the point remains: with growth, we leave some old order behind—large or small, personal or professional—and take up a new one.

TRANSFORMATION THEMES

Before examining the patterns of these transformations, three themes which are integral to growth and transition need to be introduced.

Resistance

A person does not easily leave accustomed ways of thinking, feeling, and doing things. Some *resistance* is bound to exist. We may laugh at the story of the drunk who searched for his keys not where he lost them but under a street lamp where the light was good. However, don't we all have this drunk within us with regard to change? Our old world is where the light is best, and most of us, no matter how wise and mature, are a little afraid of the dark. After all, the dark impedes seeing what we're doing. Also, some bogeyman might get us. Who knows what might happen? Who wants to be out there in the dark? Or, as Woody Allen has said, "It's not that I'm afraid of dying; I just don't want to be there when it happens." Shakespeare's Hamlet put it this way (1961, p. 920):

> Who would fardels bear
> To grunt and sweat under a weary life,
> But that the dread of something after death,
> The undiscover'd country from whose bourn
> No traveller returns, puzzles the will
> And makes us rather bear those ills we have
> Than fly to others that we know not of?

So, we tend to stay under the street lamp of our old worlds.

Grief

Life and death imagery is not too strong in talking about growth. With transformation, an old order dies, and a new one is born. Whether growth involves a small part of us or our whole personhood, a loss occurs before the gain. This realization brings us to the *grieving* which is often associated with growth, a phenomenon which is frequently overlooked, or at best underestimated. A book about growth would perform a disservice not to mention the grief that people commonly feel over the loss of their old world, no matter how much they like their new one. Growth is certainly one of the peak experiences of life, but like life itself, growth has its pain as well as its pleasure. After all, a time probably existed when the old order worked for us. These times stand like beacons in our memories as we leave familiar harbors and set sail for new ones. The depth of our grief usually depends on the magnitude of our transformation. With major growth—transformation which involves the core of our person—major grief often occurs. With minor growth—transformation in a small, relatively contained part of ourselves—only minor, perhaps imperceptible grief occurs. We are most vulnerable to this grief when we are between worlds, having left the old but not yet arrived at the new. Each of us has our own style of handling loss, and we need to recognize our grieving style and realize that we will probably use it in our growth projects.

Courage

As we can see, *courage* is involved in growth. We must leave the old world and set out to discover the new world without, as the philosopher John Dewey put it earlier, "guarantee in advance for what it shall be, or...what the new world shall do to [us] when it comes" (1958, p. 246). Naturally, the risk intimidates us. Few among us consider ourselves to be courageous, but we do act courageously from time to time. Some of the most powerful and inspiring experiences in my life have involved watching "normal" people manage their fear and grief in order to move on to a new world. I remember when my father died, which was a tremendous blow to all of us, how each member of the family fought bravely to move forward and to grow from the untimely and tragic loss. We were not mental super-stars, but somewhere we found the courage. I'm sure that we are not unusual in that respect. And this fact heartens me to no end. Everyday, I see individual acts of courage regarding growth. Along with all of the human frailties, people possess a certain toughness. Call it a survival instinct if you wish, or call it courage. But whatever you call it, this strength is essential to growth. We need it as we set out like Christopher Columbus for our New Worlds. This courage required by growth is well within the limits of most of us. We usually aren't as bad as we think we are. As psychologist and people-enthusiast Leo Buscaglia put it, "You can't be wrong all the time...even a clock that stops is right twice a day!"

TRANSFORMATION PATTERNS

With these three themes as an introduction—*resistance* to leaving the old world, *grieving* over its loss, and *courage* to risk the loss and forge a new world—we will now move on to the various patterns of transition in which these growth-related phenomena occur. Remember that development-as-growth involves *adding* new things to ourselves, *integrating* them with what was there before, and as a result, *transforming* some large or small aspect of ourselves, perhaps even our whole being. Patterns to this process do exist. These patterns will tend to occur whether or not we allow for them. However, the sequences pass more constructively and less painfully, if we make room for them in planning growth projects for ourselves and for others, as opposed to just barging ahead naively. Remaining ignorant of developmental phases, or lacking respect for them, encourages unrealistic expectations and sets the stage for disappointment and frustration, not two of the more desirable outcomes of trying to manage growth.

Pattern 1: Between Transformations

First of all, growth involves some kind of transition, and periods of transition seem to alternate with periods of stability. Rather than following a strict linear pattern:

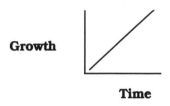

Growth

Time

growth seems to upsurge between plateaus of stability:

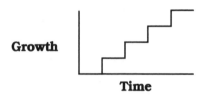

Growth

Time

One of the striking features about the various literatures on change is that this alternating pattern occurs in each of them. Whether we are talking about general systems, individuals, or groups, we see that dramatic change is usually followed by a period of stability and incorporation.

Even in whole communities, this pattern holds true. For example, in Thomas Kuhn's influential book, *The Structure of Scientific Revolutions* (1970), the world view of scientific communities are shown to undergo alternating periods of "revolution" and "normalcy." Just like the rest of us, scientists have frames of reference—certain beliefs, attitudes, and values—which shape their realities. These frames of reference—or what Kuhn calls "paradigms"—draw out certain parts of the world as worthy of attention. These paradigms influence the kinds of questions which scientists ask about their worlds, and guide the way in which scientists answer these questions. Paradigms are related directly to the accepted theories of the day. No theory is perfect, and "anomalies"—phenomena which do not fit the theory—occur occasionally. Often anomalies aren't even noticed, since frames of reference, or paradigms, tend to screen out that which does not support them. When the anomalies *are* noticed, they are usually rationalized away or somehow discredited. These patterns are features of relatively stable periods. "We have a world view which works fairly well, and don't tell anyone I said this, but don't rock the boat!" Resistance to change is high. In 1873, in *Physics and Politics*, Walter Bagehot made a pertinent observation which still holds true:

> One of the greatest pains to human nature is the pain of a new idea. It...makes you think that after all, your favorite notions my be wrong, your firmest beliefs ill-founded.... Naturally, therefore, common men hate a new idea, and are disposed more or less to ill-treat the original man who brings it. (p. 169)

After a while, however, the anomalies pile up, and the fact that the paradigm isn't working anymore becomes indisputable. Then crisis occurs, until someone comes along with a bright idea which forms the basis of a new paradigm. A dramatic transformation results at this point—a "paradigm shift" or "revolution." The new paradigm must be able to explain the known phenomena, but also, it must leave plenty of unanswered questions. It must be strict enough to eliminate neatly the anomalies which have appeared, but loose enough to capture the imagination and creativity of the adopting scientists. "I do believe that this is it! But it needs to be tested further, and developed. We'll need to start some experiments right away!" And off they go into another period of stability, working out the ramifications of the new paradigm.

Sound familiar?! Kuhn could have been describing one of us as we work out our own growth. The way in which our framework for growth fits such a wide variety of scales continues to impress me. Something is added and integrated, then transformation occurs. Whether we are talking about our backhands in tennis, our whole person, our families, our organizations, or our professional communities, the same pattern seems to hold true. Resistance, grieving, courage, these themes appear to be omnipresent to some degree as well.

Anyway, the point which I am making is that transformation is not continuous. Fallow periods seem to exist between the periods of growth.

The presence of this typical rhythm does not mean that we cannot always be involved in a growth project of some sort. The pattern simply requires that we select the object of our growth very carefully. Remember that the person can be thought of as a mind/body system with various formal and functional properties. Also, recall that within this overall system, a multitude of subsystems exist in a rough hierarchy. Our definition of development-as-growth can apply to any part of us, as well as to our whole person. Recognizing that transformation seems to need to alternate with stability requires us to avoid fixating on one particular aspect or scale of ourselves, or others, for relentless, unbroken growth. This kind of hammering concentration is profoundly counterproductive. We need to move around with our developmental attention. If we have been focusing on our whole person, perhaps we need to shift to a developmental project which is relatively narrow—learning to use computers, for example. If we have been concentrating on skills which are important to our intimate relationships, perhaps we should shift our attention to the parts of us which have more to do with our professional competence. If we have been doing a lot of mind work, maybe we should zero in on our bodies for a while. And so forth. Transition, stability, transition, stability—the pattern can be respected without forsaking a general growth orientation.

In my classes, some participants commonly remark that they have been doing a great deal of growing lately and that they feel a need to rest. We've all had this feeling before. Usually, these people have been working on some major aspect of themselves. As we talk further, we realize that they do not really want to stop growing, but rather, that they want time to stabilize their growth in whatever areas on which they've been working. Typically, they have been adding great heaps of self-awareness and integrating the new knowledge into their self-concepts. They need time to let the transformations gell and to allow themselves and the people around them to become comfortable with their new selves. Now is not a time for any more massive transformations. But they consistently light up at the prospect of growth in relatively narrow aspects of themselves. The idea of growth still excites them. For example, this time might be when they choose to begin an exercise program in order to become more skilled at managing their own conditioning. Having a growth orientation is really a way of life—a very *desirable* way of life—and placing a moratorium on all growth for people who have this orientation usually not only produces an uncomfortable boredom but also is highly disorienting. "Things just don't seem right. I thought that I needed a rest. But I feel antsy and sluggish all at the same time. It's weird!" These feelings may be weird, but they are not surprising. A basic orientation has been changed from growth to maintenance. No wonder the person feels strange. This switch is a big transition for a "rest" period! This kind of "weirdness" can be avoided by simply *shifting the attention of our growth-work*—out of respect for the transition/stability pattern—without *forsaking our overall growth orientation.* Recognizing the transition/stability pattern helps to make this kind of planning possible.

Pattern 2: Within Transformations

Now we know the context of transformation: it sits between periods of relative stability. But what about the transformation itself...do phases appear within it? Is a pattern present which is useful for us to know? Such a pattern does seem to exist.

William Bridges has provided a wonderful service in his book, *Transitions* (1980), by describing the three phases which seem to characterize life transitions: *endings, the neutral zone,* and *new beginnings.* His framework is based on the work of Arnold van Gennep, a Dutch anthropologist, who around the turn of the century studied the transition rituals of tribal societies. In van Gennep's famous work, *Rites of Passage* (1960), he identified three phases which each of these ceremonies seemed to manifest: separation, transition, and incorporation. Bridges sensitively adapted these concepts to personal transitions in modern society and used them to arrange a discussion of coping strategies which had emerged from his teaching, research, and own personal journey.

Growth is a kind of transition. It involves a transformation which results from adding and integrating new things within ourselves. As a kind of transition, therefore, growth experiences also can be seen to have these three phases: endings, the neutral zone, and new beginnings.

Endings are a time of realizing that our old ways don't work as well as we would like, and of letting go of the frame of reference which is centered on these old ways. Often, the need for change is impressed upon us by some kind of "trigger event"—a death, divorce, birth, promotion...something which makes us recognize that our old perspective won't cut it anymore and that we need to give it up. Bridges talked about the four D's of endings: disengagement, disidentification, disenchantment, and disorientation. Whether or not we have chosen the endings, they are a time of leaving the old world behind...for where, we aren't quite sure yet.

Endings can come in many forms, and our psychological reactions to them are just as varied. In general, our response can be estimated by where a particular ending falls on the following five continua:

1. **Major-Minor**

   Does the change involve a central part of our being? Or a peripheral aspect?

2. **Anticipated-Unanticipated**

   Did we expect the change (aging, for example)? Or was the change a surprise?

3. **Planned-Unplanned**

   Did we consciously choose the change, or not?

4. **Gradual-Eruptive**

   Did the change develop slowly? Or did it come out of the blue?

5. **Positive-Negative**

   Were we actually kind of glad the change occurred? Or was it a terrible blow?

Typically, endings are easier for people if they are minor, anticipated, planned, gradual, and positive, and harder if they are major, unanticipated, unplanned, eruptive, and negative.

We need to note here that although endings can be made *easier,* especially through a proactive approach such as we are developing in this book, they are rarely altogether *easy.* Leaving the security of the known world—no matter how horrible—for the insecurity of exploring a new world is simply difficult. Most people like things to be predictable, and risking is unnerving. Also, at some level, we recognize that creating a new world is an immense amount of work.

In the past, when I have made this point about the difficulty of endings, a few people have said, "But I like change and risk...it's exciting!" However, talking further has revealed that these people are usually not changing as much as they think that they are, or risking much of anything. For example, take the young man we mentioned earlier who was always changing relationships. He found endings rather comfortable, even exhilarating on the surface. But, if you recall, this kind of change fell into the category of change-but-no-change. *"Plus ça change, plus c'est la même chose"* ("the more things change, the more they stay the same"). The women in his life changed, but his relationship pattern stayed the same. The mild euphoria over leaving came from yet again saving his pattern from change. Unfortunately, his pattern did not produce a lasting happiness in him, and he was coming to realize that a transformation was necessary. He needed, and wanted, to learn to commit to someone besides himself. The old way was not working, and he needed to leave it behind. With much resistance, he summoned the courage to move on, but not without major grieving over the loss of his old world.

We need to recognize that this young man is in us all, and that putting an end to our accustomed ways is not easy for anyone. Anticipating this difficulty and understanding that endings are merely a phase of growth helps us tremendously in moving forward constructively. We realize that we are not alone, that our difficulty is a natural, human response. And we can take comfort in the fact that this too shall pass. With these reassurances, we can more easily concentrate our energies on the tasks at hand: grieving wisely and preparing for the voyage to the new world. Without them, we waste time with meta-level worries: "Should I be feeling this?" "Does anyone else feel this way?" "Am I going nuts?" Yes, you should feel resistant to leaving the old world. Yes, other people react the same way. No, you're not going nuts, but you might if you keep worrying about it.

Following endings, we move into the neutral zone. We have said goodbye, but not yet said hello. We are in transit between worlds...at sea, sailing but not yet arrived. Initially becoming seasick is common. The water heaves before us, behind us, beside us, everywhere, waves upon swells, and deep, dark troughs. Nothing is solid and fixed. We stand at the helm undaunted, but nauseous, or lie below in our cabin, turning green. Finally, we surrender to the motion, the lack of stability, and become one with it. Then, we get our sea legs and can concentrate on the voyage.

In the neutral zone, a special skill is required: tolerance of ambiguity. We don't like ambiguity much, especially in this culture. We prefer a sense of order. We want to have an intelligible pattern to our lives so that we have a basis for action. And being able to act is very important to Americans. Hanging loose is hard for us. We feel vulnerable and weak. Psychologists have well demonstrated this need for order in what are called "non-contingent reward experiments" (incidentally, for a very readable discussion of this type of research, see Watzlawick, 1976, pp. 45-54). In these studies, people are asked to solve a set of problems, but whether or not they are told that they have arrived at the correct solution is not contingent on the answer which they give. Instead, the researchers decide in advance what the subjects will be told, regardless of their response. When the subjects get it "right," sometimes they are told that they are correct, and sometimes incorrect. The same routine is followed when the subjects get it "wrong." In other words, no pattern is available to the subjects for determining what is right and wrong. The odd thing is that in post-test interviews most people have discerned some pattern to guide their responses. They feel that they have the problem "figured out." The brighter the people, the more elaborate are the patterns. Kind of frightening, isn't it?! The ramifications of these findings can be far-reaching. Some skeptics even extend the implications to the domain of theology. I don't know about that application. But I do know that in this culture we prefer order over ambiguity.

The neutral zone requires us to embrace ambiguity for a time and to become tolerably comfortable with it. We can do this more easily if we realize that everyone experiences this phase, and that it has some very important functions in our growth process. For one thing, the relative emptiness of the neutral zone enables us to see things anew without the filters of the old world. People often report a sense of heightened awareness during this phase. Fresh perceptions occur; new insights come; and unrecognized options emerge.

Secondly, during the ambiguity of the neutral zone, we deepen our appreciation of the value and function of a sound frame of reference. Lacking one, we come to understand better just what a frame of reference is. This enables us to become more competent at shaping our own world views.

Thirdly, having a time of ambiguity releases us to experiment with new ways. This exploration is something which is difficult when we have a lot at stake in preserving our old worlds. Being between worlds, however, gives us the opportunity to try out all sorts of "exotica," often with the unexpected finding that previously unacceptable things work quite nicely after all. The things which we add to our old ways as a part of the growth process often come from this kind of experimentation.

And finally, the neutral zone gives us the time to integrate our new learnings. We have trouble leaving time for these new syntheses, instead preferring to leap from the old ways to the new. As we grow, we add new learnings, but growth does not occur without the integration which produces the transformation in us. We need to allow space for it. The neutral zone is the phase in which this integration can occur.

As we can see, we need the neutral zone in order to shape our new worlds. Besides that, the phase is going to come whether we want it or not. We need to accept it and put it to good use.

The final phase of growth—new beginnings—is a time for situating our transformation within ourselves and our relationships. We have added new learnings and integrated them with the old order so as to transform the whole which was the object of our growth, whether it was some part of ourselves or our entire being. We need time to incorporate this newness and to let others adjust to it. *The new beginnings phase is a period of spinning out the ramifications of our transformation and getting used to them.*

Remember that earlier we made the point that a person can be seen to be a system, or whole, which is made up of a vast number of sub-systems, or smaller wholes, arranged in a loose hierarchy. The person—a *whole*—is also a *part* of larger systems, such as family, organization, community, nation, and so forth. Recognizing this interconnectedness helps us to see the possibility, even likelihood, of ripple effects from our various transformations.

The new beginnings phase provides the opportunity for these ripple effects to work themselves out. A transformation in one part of us may be, at a higher level, a substantial addition which needs to be integrated and thereby may cause a significant transformation at that other level. Similarly, a transformation of our whole personhood may cause important additions to the systems which comprise our relationships. These additions may need to be integrated within our existing relationships and so may cause a transformation of these systems. This rippling out needs time, and the new beginning is the phase during which it can occur.

For example, recall the woman we mentioned previously who discovered in her late thirties that her husband had had an affair. She experienced an ending to the way in which she had thought and felt about a major part of her life: her marriage. She remained committed to the relationship, but she knew that things would never be the same again. Her marriage had many good things, and she wanted to preserve them; however, she recognized that she needed a new perspective for herself and her marriage. Just what that new perspective was to be she had no idea. She entered the neutral zone. During this phase, she went back to college to finish her baccalaureate degree. Her objectives were to accomplish some much needed personal exploration as well as to acquire the learning and credentials which would help her to earn a living for herself in case it ever became necessary. In the process of her studies, she integrated her new learning with what she already knew in order to forge a new, more competent self. She also did quite well academically, and went on to a master of social work program as a second step in initiating a promising career in human services. With these developments, she moved into the beginnings phase of her growth. In this phase, she found that her tasks involved continuing to work on integrating the spinoff effects within herself of her new self-concept, as well as helping her husband and her children to integrate her profound transformations. This story is not uncommon for re-entry women. However, it also typifies the function of the new beginnings phase of growth regardless of who we are.

Before closing this discussion of the phases of the growth process, two important points need to be made. First of all, caution is in order regarding the way in which we think about the endings phase. Endings do not involve chucking everything and starting from scratch. This drastic measure is not only impossible, but also the attempt can be terribly destructive to ourselves and to those around us. I feel an ethical responsibility to make this point strongly. Growth involves adding to ourselves, and through the integration of these various new things, transforming ourselves. Growth builds on our previous experiences; it does not try to eradicate them. These experiences are within us, whether we like it or not, and repressing them usually leads to harm. Integrating them constructively leads to growth, for as the saying goes which Robert Lovett shared with Robert Kennedy during the Cuban missile crisis, "Good judgment is usually the result of experience. And experience is frequently the result of bad judgment" (Schlesinger, 1978, p. 555).

The transformation of growth takes the whole which we were and changes it to a new synthesis of a substantially different quality. Elements of the old exist within the new. Our lives have threads of continuity. Thank goodness! The phrase "endings" does not mean that we snip these threads. Rather, it means that the whole tapestry which the various elements of ourselves constitute is changing its form as we weave in new elements.

In the endings phase, we need to avoid stigmatizing the elements of our old lives and shunning them completely in making our transformation. This kind of prejudice not only can lead us to ignore many valuable features of ourselves and our social networks, but also, it can significantly stunt the integration processes of our growth, both in ourselves and in our relationships. Remember the women we mentioned in our sex role discussion who tried to add "male" qualities while *subtracting* "female" qualities, instead of *integrating* the two together. The strategy didn't work well at all and was quite painful for them and the people around them. Endings involve the termination of the whole but not the elimination of all of its elements.

A second point worth making about these three transition phases is that the depth of their impact on us is directly related to the magnitude of the growth project in which we are involved. The more central the growth is to the core of our being, the more noticeable will be the impact of these phases on our overall experience; the less central, the less noticeable. This pattern means that if we are engaged in relatively minor growth projects, we do not need to anticipate major grieving over our endings, profound emptiness in our neutral zones, or vast ripple effects in our new beginnings. We may not even be aware of the three phases if the growth is minor enough. One of the exciting features of our definition of growth is that it can be used equally well for any magnitude of growth project. Those of us who have relatively small and well-contained growth projects in mind, as opposed to large-scale, personal transformation, need not worry that we are risking major upset as we embark on our growth.

Usefulness of Knowing Transformation Patterns

Before closing this chapter, the value of knowing these various developmental phases bears summarizing. First of all, being aware of these frameworks helps us to remember that we are not alone in the experiences we have as we make our transitions. We can take comfort in the fact that we are not weird, rather than dissipating our energies by worrying about whether we should be feeling what we are feeling. Secondly, the frameworks can help to give us hope because we know what is coming up and that eventually the new beginning will arrive, for as Friedrich Nietzsche commented, "He who has a *why* to live for can bear almost any *how*." (Frankl, 1963, p. 121). Thirdly, being aware of the necessary sequence of phases encourages us to allow time for each phase and to plan accordingly. This awareness provides us with a basis for patience to let current growth projects work themselves out, and a foundation for the wisdom to know when and in what aspect of ourselves to initiate new growth projects. And finally, knowing about transition patterns helps us to concentrate on developing the resources and strategies to pass constructively through the various phases. We know just what we are working on at any particular time, and this knowledge provides us with a very useful problem-solving focus.

So, we close Part I of our explorations having clarified what we mean when we are talking about growth. In Parts II and III, we will examine ten specific qualities—five within the environment and five within ourselves—which seem to promote growth. From this discussion, some concrete ideas will emerge which should help us a great deal in developing effective strategies and resources in order to accomplish the objectives of our consciously-chosen growth projects.

Marshall McLuhan once remarked that we are "driving into the future while looking out of the rearview mirror" (Kanter, 1983, p. 62). However, with our theory of development, we have added significantly to our ability to look forward and to plan our course wisely.

PART II

WHAT CAN THE ENVIRONMENT CONTRIBUTE?

We never educate directly, but indirectly by means of the environment. Whether we permit chance environments to do the work, or whether we design environments for the purpose makes a great difference. And any environment is a chance environment so far as its educative influence is concerned unless it has been deliberately regulated with reference to its educative effect.

John Dewey, *Democracy and Education* (1944, p. 19)

...to excite individuals' awareness and realization of humanity's higher potentials I seek through comprehensive anticipatory design science...to reform the environment instead of trying to reform humans....

R. Buckminister Fuller, "What I Am Trying To Do" (1973, p. 5)

Development-as-growth results from the interaction of the *person* and the *environment*. We cannot extricate ourselves from all environments and go away to grow. We will always be in some context which will influence the nature of our experience. Nor can we simply rely on our surroundings to produce growth in us. What we bring to any particular situation as unique personalities will always play an important role in shaping the experience which we have there. As noted earlier, we are neither Super-beings, who are capable of willing any deed regardless of the circumstances, nor automotons, which respond in a predictable way to certain environmental stimuli.

Within the two main participants of the fundamental interaction—the person and the environment—elements exist which encourage growth, as well as those which discourage it. When growth occurs, it emerges from the interplay of these various positive and negative forces. A primary task in planning and accomplishing growth projects—which is our main interest in this book—is to try to maximize the features which encourage growth, while minimizing those which discourage it. Toward this end, Part II will focus on managing the environment of growth, while Part III will deal with the person and what he or she brings to that environment.

In establishing a definition of development, Part I laid the groundwork for *objective-setting* and *evaluation*—knowing what we are trying to do, and when we have done it. Building on this definition, Parts II and III will take up the other two important elements of the planning process: *strategies* and *resources*— determining how we plan to achieve our objectives, and what we need to help us to do so.

In the next section, Part II, we will examine five characteristics of the environment which encourage development: *novelty, minimal threat, supportiveness of the learning cycle, information richness,* and *learning facilitators.* In separate chapters, we will explore why each particular characteristic removes barriers to growth and promotes it, as well as ways in which we can work these elements into specific projects. From these discussions will come concrete ideas concerning resources and strategies for achieving our developmental objectives.

This list of features which promote development is not meant to be exhaustive. Others exist no doubt, and you should feel free to add your own. However, these five environmental characteristics do provide a handy, beginning checklist of things to think about in formulating specific growth projects. If the features are present in an environment, they do not guarantee growth, but they do seem to encourage it, as will become clear in the following chapters.

Objectives for Part II: To explore five environmental features which promote development, and to improve our skills at actualizing them in day-to-day living.

CHAPTER 7

NOVELTY

Depend upon it, sir, when a man knows he is to be hanged in a fortnight, it concentrates his mind wonderfully.

Samuel Johnson (Boswell, 1980, p. 849)

For most of us, being hanged qualifies as a novel experience, and the prospect certainly would encourage us to re-think things a bit. However, we don't need to be perfectly literal about Samuel Johnson's quip. When a person encounters *any* new situation which demands sorting out, "...it concentrates his mind wonderfully." We all have our accepted ways of constructing the world and of interacting with it, and when these ways aren't working anymore, the search begins for a better order of things. From this dynamic, which is stimulated by novelty, growth can come.

AN EXAMPLE OF NOVELTY AT WORK

Let's say that a male manager begins working in an academic organization whose culture is predominantly female. Recent work has shown that thinking of organizations as cultures leads to valuable insights (e.g., Schein, 1985). Each organization can be seen to have its own structures, roles, rituals, norms, laws, language, values, and so forth, just as larger social units which we usually think of as cultures, such as nations. We also know enough about sex role socialization to recognize that two basic gender-related orientations exist: female and male (e.g., Chodorow, 1978; Gilligan, 1982). The female orientation values nurturing, relationship-building, intuition, emotional sensitivity, collaboration, and win-win solutions, whereas the male perspective values aggressiveness, task-accomplishment, reason, cognitive competence, competition, and win-lose contexts. An organization with a female culture is one in which its various structures, systems, rituals, values, and so forth are dominated by a female perspective. In short, our male manager finds himself in an *intercultural* experience of a major magnitude.

In his first meeting, he argues firmly for his position on the initial agenda item. Enjoying a good debate, he has amassed a great deal of material in support of his argument. He has looked forward to seeing the approaches and evidence that his colleagues have prepared. From this competition of ideas, the best will win out, he believes. And in his mind, that's what is important to him—the best solution to the tasks at hand...survival of the fittest! He's ready for the contest. If "objective" analysis shows his ideas to be wanting, then so be it. The loss may sting a bit, but he can live with the minor injury. He likes this kind of competition because it gives him feedback on the quality of his thinking. He can stand to lose; he has learned a lot by losing. The winner is the organization because it gets the best idea from the fray. Anyway, this is how he construes the situation to himself.

But this first meeting in his new organization is something quite different from the meetings to which he is accustomed. No one seems to win, and no one seems to lose. Furthermore, he can't pick out the logic of the discussion. People present their views, but little critiquing of the various positions occurs. Evaluation seems to be taboo. He makes an attempt to link up some of the various positions and to analyze "dispassionately" their advantages and disadvantages. Then, really getting into it, he aggressively presents what he thinks is a sterling, on-the-spot synthesis which accommodates the strengths of all of the positions. He's exhilarated...then surprised. His speech only seems to hurt some peoples' feelings and to concern others because they appear to think that he's getting mad. So, he clams up for the rest of the meeting. He senses that keeping quiet doesn't help much either because a few people continue to glance at him anxiously, seemingly trying to determine whether or not he's upset. He feels out of place, confused, stupid, incompetent, and frustrated. He can't seem to affect the course of events in the way he wants. His accustomed role in a discussion seems nonexistent. The meeting ambles on despite the weight of his presence, and eventually, a decision is reached with which everyone appears to feel comfortable, everyone except for him, that is. He can't spot the reasoning behind the outcome. All he sees is that most of the people feel intuitively that the decision is the right one. The darn thing about the outcome is that as the months go by he recognizes that it was the best decision. Soon he comes to realize that he has his work cut out for him if he is to learn this new way of doing things. Clearly, it is worth the effort.

The hypothetical male manager has a developmental demand placed on him by the novelty of his environment. The pressure which he feels is the need to cultivate his female side. Researchers and theorists suggest that people have within them the potential for both "male" and "female" qualities (e.g., Gutmann, 1968; Jung, 1933; Neugarten & Gutmann, 1968), but as we move from infancy to adulthood, gender socialization works to encourage one set over the other. As midlife comes along, those "voices from other rooms," as writer Truman Capote put it, become louder and we respond developmentally. Men become more nurturing and relational, and women become more aggressive and autonomous. Placing a male manager in the novel culture of a female organization requires tapping this potential which life-span psychology suggests that we all have within us. The result is a person who is more fully developed, someone who is more capable of being either rational or intuitive, autonomous or relational, competitive or collaborative, cognitive or emotional, assertive or nurturing, *as appropriate.*

Incidentally, we should note that with many more women entering professions, women are more likely than men to experience the kind of developmental demand which was just described. We could even argue that men's development is systemically stunted in this regard. Most professions are dominated by male culture. This circumstance means that when women enter professions, they encounter a novel environment. Willy-nilly, they have an intercultural experience which demands that they learn a new way of being—a male way. In contrast, men do not encounter this kind of novelty when they enter the professions. The culture which they meet is precisely the culture for which they were socialized—male culture. If the women learn this new male culture and integrate it with their female perspective, they are transformed developmentally to a higher level of complexity and competence. The same opportunity is not present for men because of the lack of cultural novelty. However, just so that we don't come away with too rosy of a picture for women, we need to recognize that even though current conditions in the professions favor women over men in encountering the kind of novelty which can stimulate significant development, the supports which are so important for the actualization of development are often missing for women. Generally, male culture is at best indifferent, and at worst hostile, to the plight of these "foreigners" (for a penetrating analysis, which remains excellent even after a decade, see Kanter, 1977). So, whereas the developmental urgency produced by novelty is greater in the professions for women than for men, the developmental supports are generally lesser.

WHY NOVELTY WORKS

As we can see in this example, novelty promotes development because it creates a pressing need to change. Necessity may be the mother of development as well as of invention, the two being similar in many ways. Put in terms of our definition of growth, novelty requires that we add something to ourselves; it demands that we learn something new. With this addition, our systemic tendency to try to remain a cohesive whole (to continue being a system, to avoid "falling apart") urges us to integrate the addition within our personality, thereby creating the opportunity for a developmental transformation.

Remember the issue of resistance which we discussed earlier. Transformation is risky. Who knows what we will become, or if we will continue to exist as an integrated whole? We may not like our new self; our social worlds may not like it; or we may unravel altogether. Our worlds are filled with elements which resist transformation. Novelty helps us to overcome these barriers by creating the need for transformation.

Resistance can be viewed both in terms of our personality system and in terms of the social systems of which we are a part. Novelty works in both domains to encourage growth. Internally, we recognize in a new situation that our old ways of construing reality and of being within that reality no longer work so well. Externally, our social worlds confirm our inner perception and tell us to shape up and fit in. Novelty creates a congruence between our inner and outer worlds with regard to the need to change.

APPLYING NOVELTY

How can we use these dynamics of novelty in order to manage our growth *proactivity?* At least two avenues of application exist. First, we can learn to see novel situations which are *thrust on us* as developmental opportunities rather than as unmitigated trage- dies. And second, we can learn to *create our own* novel situations. The key in both cases is to try to match up the developmental demands of the novel environment with our specific developmental objectives. Once this task is accomplished, we can go on to complete our developmental plan for the situation. Let's look at each of the two kinds of application in more detail.

Unplanned Novelty

Growth is often related to some kind of *trigger event*—some dramatic set of circumstances which creates a novel situation and requires us to cope with it. Typically, we do not choose these trigger events; they just happen to us. Sometimes we actually choose them but without fully understanding the magnitude of the impact which they will have on us, that is, without really knowing that we are choosing a trigger event. So, in a sense, the events are also thrust on us in this case, even though we may appear to be choosing them.

Trigger events may involve a loss, such as the death of a loved one, divorce, job termination, having children move away from home, or becoming seriously ill. Or, they may relate to a gain, such as a promotion, marriage, or birth. Sometimes, determining whether a trigger event is a loss or a gain is difficult. After all, gaining a marriage also means losing a single life, just as losing children to adulthood also entails gaining freedom from day-to-day parenting.

As we can see, the kinds of losses and gains which are often trigger events lie at the heart of the typical life span. Their occurrence is the rule, not the exception. This means that as each of us lives out our lives, working out our journey as best we can, we will find ourselves periodically having to cope with dramatic turns of events—that is, with novelty. How can we make these novel situations which are thrust on us—these losses and gains—into trigger events which precipitate developmental transformation?

A brief but important note is necessary before we tackle this question. As already mentioned, many of these novel situations which we find imposed on us involve a tragic loss, and thinking about how to turn these kinds of tragedies into opportunities for personal growth may seem self-centered and morally disgusting. When my father finally succumbed at age fifty-nine to lymphoma after a wrenching fifteen-month struggle, if someone would have suggested that I use the event as a growth project, I would have been tempted to clobber the person on the spot. However, I now realize that I did use the experience for substantial growth, almost at my father's beckoning. During the ordeal, I tried to be present for my father and for the other members of my family, but also I tried to discover and come to terms with the meaning of my father's life and of his death. At the end, as I sat next to his hospital bed for an hour after he stopped breathing and felt the warmth slowly leave his hand, I tried to understand these things. I experienced in a raw almost primal form the profound bond which I had with him. I could see how much of him was in me: the look, the touch, the passion, the outreaching. I could see that parts of him lived on in me, just as parts of his father lived on in him.

I began to grasp what was to me a new notion of immortality—a very tangible and concrete form of what had been to me a rather abstract and remote concept. I was a part of my father's immortality. *All of us* who knew him, were affected by him, and loved him, played a role in his immortality, or as Tennyson put it (Tennyson, 1899b, p. 179):

> Our echoes roll from soul to soul,
> and grow forever and forever.

I realized my responsibility to my father: in some way what lived on from his life was in my hands. If I loved him, I would try to make sure that what lived on was good. My father was not an angel; he was a human being. He had had his good and his bad parts. The passion which fueled his powerful love could also propel his anger. However, he was what the world calls a "good man," someone whom we are glad to have had alive so that we could enjoy the pleasure of his relationship and so that he could add his few lines to the species' story. My commitment to him became to take what was good about him and his life and to try to help it to achieve its potential in me and in the world. The point which I am making here is that when tragedy strikes, trying to learn from it is not necessarily selfish. In some crucial way, we owe the effort to each other. From trying to help ourselves and others to grow, we can actualize the potential which has been given to us by past generations as well as add significantly to the potential of future generations. Growth need not be self-serving.

Growth occurs within the context of relationships without which no self exists. *Why* we want to grow is the important thing...for ourselves only, or for our contributions to others? From a relational perspective, trying to grow from tragedy is really a profound responsibility of human love rather than a brazen excess of self-indulgence.

With this in mind, let's return to the question before us and see how we can make novel situations which are thrust on us into developmental opportunities. The key lies in identifying the range of demands which these novel situations make on us, and then, in generating personal growth objectives which satisfy these demands. From these objectives a growth plan can be built which not only helps us to develop but also helps us to adapt to the new situation. Through this process, we achieve a potent *congruence* between our coping and our growth orientations. This unity of purpose makes the actualization of growth much easier.

First, we need to determine the demands of our new circumstances. Just what does the environment require of us in order to adapt? We need to be as specific as possible in answering this question. For example, the full-time mother who watches her last child move out of the house and take a job in another city faces what is to her a dramatically different situation: daily life without children. She could just say that things are different and leave the construal at that, as she struggles somewhat blindly with her misery. But being specific helps. Her new circumstances give her large amounts of time to fill. Hours are no longer consumed by attending games and concerts, doing huge quantities of laundry, talking through adolescent problems on a day-to-day basis, and so forth. Her new situation finds her without meaningful work, and she experiences a vacuum of purpose. She had been a *MOTHER*, but now she feels as if she is only a wife to a man who in a strange way she doesn't know very well because their separate worlds of home and office have kept them apart so much. Her new environment seems to require that she re-negotiate her relationships with her husband and her children, as well as with herself. Her oldest daughter is now pregnant, and she will soon be a grandmother. The world around her seems to be telling her that she is older. And she begins to feel it.

The second task is to take these demands and to transform the most important of them into developmental objectives. For instance, the mother in our example might settle on four areas of transformation: her approach to her own life span, her work, her marriage, and her parenting. Her objectives might include trying to add and integrate knowledge about the typical changes which people go through during the course of their lives and how her own life fits, or doesn't fit, within these general patterns. In the career area, initially she may take on re-thinking her conception of work and how it relates to her. Then, she might set out to learn about the kinds of work which she likes to do and does well, and what she needs to do in order to land a job which matches her strengths, preferences, values, and aspirations. With regard to her husband and her children, her objective may be to reconstruct each set of relationships and her role within it—a "second marriage" with her husband, and an "adult" relationship with her children. In each developmental area, she will add things—new knowledge, perspectives, skills—and then integrate them with what she was before. From this addition and integration will come the transformation which will signify her growth. Once the objectives are framed, then the resources and strategies can be determined in order to bring about the desired transformations. Classes can be lined up, counselors contacted, activities planned, support networks established, and so forth.

To summarize, at least three steps exist in making novel situations which are thrust on us into events which trigger our growth:

1. Identifying the demands which the new environment makes on us,

2. Translating the most important of these demands into personal growth objectives, and

3. Generating a growth plan (resources, strategies, evaluation, and timeline) which will accomplish these objectives.

Through this process, we take what could be a strictly *reactive* response to a new situation—just getting by as best we can with our existing way of being—and make our approach *proactive*— attempting to transform ourselves self-consciously into a new personally-chosen way of being.

Planned Novelty

As we move on, we should note that in this first avenue of applying the dynamics of novelty in order to promote growth, environmental change has come first, then our growth objectives. In the second type of application, *the reverse occurs*, the objectives come first, then environmental change follows. In other words, novelty is *introduced* in order to achieve our objectives.

Success with tis type of application involves at least three steps:

1. Clarifying our developmental objectives,

2. Identifying some novel environments which would require us to achieve these objectives as a part of our environmental adaptation, and

3. Incorporating one (or more) of these novel situations into our specific growth plan.

Once again, we can see that this procedure taps the considerable energy of our adaptive response—our need to survive in a new situation—and puts that drive to work in service of our growth interests. With this process, we achieve that highly desirable congruence of our coping and growth orientations.

Let's look at some examples of how we might use this procedure. Say for instance that we want to develop our leadership skills, not only because of their general utility and benefits to our self-concept but also, thinking practically, because promotions are often dependent on them. Perhaps some of us have been supervisors and want to make the move to mid-level management. Or perhaps some of us have been teachers and hope to begin making the transitions upward through the various levels of academic administration. Maybe some of us have been counselors in agencies and want to shift our career focuses to human service management. Or maybe some of us have been housewives for fifteen years and want or need to re-enter the paid labor force at a position of responsibility (and at least moderate pay). For whatever reasons, let's say that we want to develop our ability to be a leader in organizations. With this objective in mind, we can then begin to think of various situations which *require* us to use leadership skills. In other words, we try to identify circumstances in which the environmental demands match our developmental objectives. For example, we might finally give in to requests and agree to chair a committee in some organization which is outside of our professional domain—in a church, community, or political group, perhaps. This approach has the advantage of leaving our professional reputation intact as we are learning our new skills. Threat is thereby decreased, which as we will see in the next chapter helps development along considerably. With the new environment having been chosen, we can then go on to formulate a concrete growth plan in terms of that specific environment knowing that this plan will tend to serve our larger developmental objective of acquiring transferable leadership skills.

Similarly, let's say that we want to develop our empathic skills—our ability to enter into another person's reality and participate in it actively and effectively. Perhaps this skill is important for our professional endeavors. Some of us may be teachers, counselors, ministers, salespeople, or managers—professionals for whom knowing what other people are thinking and feeling is crucial. Or perhaps empathy is significant to us in our personal relationships—for example, with our spouses, children, relatives, and friends. Again, for whatever reason, we want to develop our ability to be sensitive to the diverse ways in which people construct their worlds and relate to them.

Too often, we may find ourselves assuming that other people are like us and, consequently, suffer the disasters of miscommunication. So, we look for environments in which we need to attend to the differences in other people's realities, environments in which we cannot easily get away with a naive ego-centrism. We may discover, for example, that a superb way to create this kind of situation is to go to another culture. In this kind of setting, the differences in world views are not subtle; they rush at us from the instant we step off of the plane. We may need to attend to different realities simply to get our basic needs met...perhaps just to get our luggage. By utilizing the dynamics of this novelty, our annual vacation can turn into a profound growth project, if we plan it correctly (elements of good planning will be discussed as we proceed through the book). Of course, actually living in another culture for an extended length of time works even better. I know this to be true from my own personal experience of living for a year in Guadalajara with a Mexican family. Whether we spend a year or a week in the new culture, the important thing is that we have placed ourselves in an environment which requires us to do that which we are striving to learn how to do—that is, the environmental demands are congruent with our developmental objectives. Once again, our growth plan related to this particular environment contributes to our larger developmental aim.

On a smaller scale of growth, we may desire to develop our computer competence. Whether because our work requires it, or because we simply want to understand better the computer wizards who happen to be our children—for whatever reason, we may want to develop our comfort and facility with computers. We may select a good, hands-on computer class as an environment which demands us to do what we desire to learn to do. Our specific growth plan relating to this course then contributes to our overall growth objective. Of course, high quality, practical courses can provide this service for a wide variety of developmental objectives: life planning, relationship skills, personal growth, weight loss, public speaking, financial planning, contract bridge, and on and on—for large or small, personal or professional objectives.

The potential examples are legion, but the concepts which they illustrate are relatively few...and simple. In summary, novelty in our environment puts adaptive demands on us. If we line up these demands with our chosen developmental objectives—whether the novelty is imposed on us or we introduce it—the specific growth which we desire is more likely.

The dynamics of novelty can be a powerful tool for the growth-agent. However, novelty's power must be used with care because too much newness may threaten us, and with too much threat, we can become more closed than questing. In the next chapter, we turn to this other side of the novelty issue—the need to minimize threat.

CHAPTER **8**

MINIMIZING THREAT

A sound of cornered-animal fear and hate and surrender and definance...
like the last sound the treed and shot and falling animal makes as the dogs
get him, when he finally doesn't care any more about anything but himself
and his dying.

Ken Kesey, *One Flew Over the*
Cuckoo's Nest (1962, p. 267)

Remember the adage, "Sink or swim." The grim father, after having examined his conscience for the purity of his motives ("this hurts me more than it does him"), plucks the terrified boy from the dock and casts him into the lake, whereupon the child miraculously begins to swim like Johnny Weissmuller. Later the child thanks Daddy for having given him that push, shove, heave-ho, into the drink when he needed it.

Pretty hard to swallow, right? Threatening people does not appear to open them up to growth. As a matter of fact, it seems to get in the way.

In the last chapter, novelty was championed as an important tool for the growth-agent. But we need to recognize that putting ourselves in new situations can be threatening. After all, the reason why novelty works is that we don't work, and being dysfunctional can be a little unsettling!

Growth thrives on a proper balance of *challenge* and *support.* Novelty can provide the challenge, but what about the support? In the next four chapters, we will investigate how to introduce supports into the environment as we plan and implement various growth projects.

In this chapter, we will look at threat—why it interferes with growth, and how we can systematically minimize its presence and its destructive effect. In particular, we will examine four steps to reducing threat and managing it when it does appear.

WHY THREAT INTERFERES

One way in which to understand threat better is to explore the needs which it places in jeopardy. So to begin, let's briefly summarize Abraham Maslow's well-known theory of human needs (Maslow, 1987, pp. 15-23). Maslow has grouped human needs into a hierarchy which consists of five categories. He has concluded that we do not orient ourselves toward fulfilling level two needs until the needs at level one have been met; level three, not until levels one and two have been satisfied; and so forth. Or as Confucious put it,

> ...I have never yet seen anyone whose desire to build up his moral power was as strong as sexual desire.(Waley, 1938, p. 142)

At level one, Maslow placed physiological needs; level two, safety needs; level three, belongingness and love needs; level four, esteem needs; and level five, self-actualization needs.

Need fulfillment is of course a powerful motivation in us. The word motivation comes from the Latin root *movere*, meaning "to move." Our motivations not only cause us to move, but they provoke us to move *toward* something. In the case of needs, they direct us toward the gratification of a particular need. Motivations direct the nature of our mental states. What is relevant to us becomes that which is related to satisfying our need. Of all of the things to which we can give our attention, we give it to that which is relevant to us. The need, depending on how severe, can come to structure our perception of our worlds toward its fulfillment. Maslow cited the example of hunger (a level one, physiological need):

> For our chronically and extremely hungry person, Utopia can be defined simply as a place where there is plenty of food. He or she tends to think that, if only guaranteed food for the rest of life, he or she will be perfectly happy and will never want anything more. Life itself tends to be defined in terms of eating. Anything else will be defined as unimportant. Freedom, love, community feeling, respect, philosophy, may all be waved aside as fripperies that are useless, since they fail to fill the stomach. Such a person may fairly be said to live by bread alone.(Maslow, 1987, p. 17)

This power of needs to shape our realities deserves respect.

Growth projects are often directed at fulfilling our higher level needs. However, if lower level needs are threatened by the situations which we meet as we make our way toward growth, then we find ourselves distracted. First things first. For example, before we can concentrate on self-actualization, we feel the urge to make sure that our lower level needs are gratified. Postponing self-actualizing growth due to threat is not uncommon. Usually, we wait until we are out of the pickle before we try to make sense of it, if we ever try at all after such trauma. So, this is one reason why threat should be minimized; *its distracting.*

Another reason involves two concepts which were developed earlier: reactivity and proactivity. In the reactive mode, the person's goal is maintenance—self-protection, trying to keep things together, survival. In the proactive mode, the person's goal is transformation—opening up, trying to expand, growth. Proactivity is the fair wind of the growth-agent. However, as mentioned previously, it does require courage—the fortitude to move forward towards our growth objective and to avoid reversing our course for a familiar, albeit undesirable, harbor. C. K. Chesterton called courage "a contradiction in terms," when he described it as involving "a strong desire to live taking the form of readiness to die" (Prochnow & Prochnow, 1962, p. 60). Along these lines, an old saying advises us, "Courage is not freedom from fear; it is being afraid and going on." I believe that each of us is courageous in our own way, but even so, I think that we all have our limits. Managing our fear or anxiety—no matter how strong and clever we are—is taxing, and sooner or later, we can simply exhaust our courage. At this point of debilitation, we enter the reactive mode and concentrate on defending ourselves rather than reaching out and planning to get our needs met. The proactive mode is effective in need fulfillment at any level of Maslow's hierarchy. However, with too much threat, over too long a time, we lose energy and simply hang on as best we can. So, the second reason why threat should be minimized is that *it's debilitating.* Threat can deplete our courage sufficiently to shift us from proactivity to reactivity—from a transformative mode to a maintenance mode. Growth suffers as a result.

Distraction and *debilitation*—no doubt other reasons exist which explain why threat interferes with growth. However, these two should suffice to make the point that we need to try to reduce threat as much as possible as we go about planning and implementing our growth projects. We don't need to toss ourselves in the lake...sink or swim...even if that is what our Daddies did. We can be different kinds of parents with ourselves.

HOW TO MINIMIZE THREAT

So we need to try to minimize threat in planning growth projects. But how? I would like to discuss four steps which if followed can be very helpful.

Step 1: Know Your Threat Patterns

The simple point here is that different things are threatening to different people. For example, the person who likes to learn things through hands-on approaches may find it threatening to enter a situation which requires lecture-learning. And vice versa. Remember the discussion of Kolb's theory of learning styles. Kolb describes the learning cycle as having four phases: we begin with concrete experience, reflect on that experience, abstract generalizations from it, and then experiment based on our generalizations. Usually, we prefer different phases of the learning cycle over others, and from these preferences our learning style emerges. When we enter environments which value learning styles other than our preferred mode, we usually feel uncomfortable. For instance, university professors often have learning styles which emphasize abstract conceptualization more strongly than their students, many of whom are aspiring practitioners rather than would-be academicians. If the professors teach in a style in which they prefer to learn, the typical student is bound to feel a little uncomfortable. This pattern means that for the thousands of adults who are considering going back to school, either at the undergraduate or graduate level, they can expect to find the learning environments of colleges and universities to be moderately (to extremely!) threatening. At least this used to be true, I am happy to say. With the advent of "nontraditional" programs in higher education—many of which are individualized and learner-centered—educational consumers are increasingly able to shop around in order to locate programs with sophisticated teachers and curricula which show sensitivity to learning style diversity. In any event, the point stands: environments which devalue our preferred learning styles are threatening. Different learning environments will be threatening to different people, depending in this case on the degree of congruence between the preferred learning style of the person and the environment. Knowing this threat pattern helps us in selecting appropriate learning environments for our growth projects.

Once again, different things are threatening to different people. Another example can be found in the area of processing our feelings. In typical sex–role socialization, men are taught to withhold their feelings in order to be the Rock-of-Gibraltar, strong, silent type, whereas women are encouraged to be emotional specialists so as better to be the Earth Mother who is capable of monumental feats of nurturing. This pattern means that when a couple decides to enhance their marriage by undergoing human relations training together, the man is likely to be far more threatened than the woman. As the sweat begins to bead on his forehead, he is more likely to withhold inappropriately, or to disclose inappropriately. In fact, just plain inappropriate sums up the way he feels about himself in the situation. He can't seem to get the hang of it. Because of lack of practice, we would expect him to be threatened. Meanwhile, his wife feels comfortable going with the flow of the group. Her main source of discomfort comes from the things which her husband is saying, or not saying. Again, the point is that knowing what is threatening to us helps in selecting constructive environments for our growth projects.

Included in this step of knowing our threat patterns is not only awareness of what is threatening to us, and to what degree, but also cognizance of our typical response to that which threatens us. In this regard, a very useful learning instrument, called the *Strength Deployment Inventory,* has been developed by Elias Porter (1985). Of particular interest is the instrument's capacity to give us feedback about our response to stress. The inventory is based on three fundamental types of motivation concerning our relationships with others:

Altruistic-Nurturing Motivation

...trusting, optimistic, loyal, idealistic, helpful, modest, devoted, caring, supportive, accepting, adaptable...the individual places the enhancement of the welfare of others at the top of his priorities in relating to others...basic gratifications come from being nurturant of others without asking or demanding direct rewards in return....

Assertive-Directing Motivation

...self-confident, enterprising, ambitious, organizing (of others), per-suasive, forceful, quick-to-act, imaginative, challenging, proud, bold, risk-taking...the individual places the achievement of goals through in-fluencing the activities of others at the top of his priorities in relating to others...basic gratifications come from being self-assertive and directing of others....

Analytic-Autonomizing Motivation

...cautious, practical, economical, reserved, methodical, analytic, prin-cipled, orderly, fair, persevering, conserving, thorough...the individual places the achievement of self-reliance, self-sufficiency and self-depen-dence at the top of his priorities in relating to others...basic gratifications come from the achievement of self-direction and autonomy through logical analysis and judicious foresight....(Porter, 1977, p. 4)

Using various combinations of these basic types, Porter and his associates derive seven motivational orientations which may characterize us in our interpersonal relations. Now, we get to the point. The instrument shows that when we are defensive, such as when we are threatened by conflict or opposition, we often change our motivational type—or our basic orientation in our relation-ships. For example, nurturing people may become cautious and analytical. Or analytical people may become assertive and directing. What is your pattern when threatened? Taking the *Strength Deployment Inventory* might provide some useful feedback. Or perhaps you know an instrument which you like better. Even if you can't find a suitable instrument, the question is worth pursuing. Ask some people who know you well, in addition to doing your own soul-searching.

Once again, the objectives of knowing our threat patterns are to increase our awareness of *what is threatening to us* and *how we typically respond to threat.* With this knowledge, we can better accomplish Step 2 toward minimizing threat in growth projects.

Step 2: Select Novelty Which Is Not Too Threatening

You're probably thinking, "What in the world does he mean by 'too threatening?'" Good question. I would like to suggest three criteria for defining this threat threshold.

In order to reach an understanding of the first criterion, enter with me for a moment into a metaphor. In yoga, a method of developing the ability to reach the various postures—many of which appear impossible at first—is to build up our capacity through successive approximations. In attempting the posture, we come to the limits of our tendons' flexibility, then go just a little bit further, and hold it for a while. We do not go very much further than our limit, or we cause damage. However, we do stretch beyond our comfort zone...some. Through this process, our comfort zone is extended, and eventually we are able to hold the posture full-blown.

In some education circles, this approach has become known as "one-plus-one learning," after work by Jean Piaget, the well-known developmental psychologist. Using this method, students are encouraged to proceed up to the limits of their comfort zone in a particular knowledge or skill area, and then to stretch beyond that limit a bit. Not too far...otherwise regression or traumatic confusion can occur. But some. The skilled teacher not only has the judgment to sense students' limits but also encourages them to concentrate on knowing their own thresholds so as to become better self-directed learners.

The first criterion, then, for selecting novelty which is not too threatening involves choosing environments which comply with the one-plus-one principle. Novelty is bound to be threatening. That's good. It should *urge* us to grow in order to adapt better. However, the novelty should not push us so far beyond our comfort zone that we either regress in self-protection or suffer some sort of psychological trauma as we "gut it out." The self-awareness from Step 1 regarding what is threatening to us, and to what degree, will help a great deal as we make one-plus-one judgments regarding specific environments.

The second criterion for selecting novelty which is not too threatening is also based on the self-awareness generated in Step 1. Recall Maslow's hierarchy of needs. We need to respect the tendency to deal first with the lowest level need which is threatened. That means, for example, if our physiological needs are threatened, neglecting these needs in order to focus on self-actualization would be highly unlikely.

Environments which are "too threatening" can further be defined, then, as those which jeopardize important needs which are irrelevant to the objectives of our growth project. Theoretically, developmental objectives can focus on any need level. Let's say that we wish to concentrate on our esteem needs by aiming to develop a more positive self-concept. Perhaps we have always wanted to feel that we could survive in the wilderness if necessary. We may value our biological heritage highly, and our self-esteem would benefit if we could prove to ourselves that we could function as competent creatures in the wild. In this case, a survival program, such as Outward Bound, might be an appropriate environment for our growth project. Sure, our lower level physiological and safety needs would be threatened. Our attention would be riveted on meeting them. But in this instance, that would be the point. By successfully meeting these lower level needs our self-esteem would increase. A congruence would exist between the needs which we place in jeopardy and the growth objectives which we wish to achieve.

This congruence would disappear, however, if the main objective of our growth project was to learn to love more construc-tively. Say, for example, that our developmental concern still focused on creating a more positive self-concept, and that the part of ourselves which bothered us the most was our ability to achieve a healthy intimacy with others. Entering a survival experience would probably not be the best growth environment for us. In such an environment, meeting our physiological and safety needs would be imperative. But also, it would be irrelevant to that which would elevate our self-esteem. Joining a human relations training seminar might be a better choice in this case.

The point of the second criterion is that we need to be sophisticated about the primacy of our various needs. Some needs demand to be met before others. What is threatening, and to what degree, will differ for each of us. However, we all tend to manifest some kind of hierarchy of needs, even if we don't agree with Maslow's groupings. Environments are "too threatening" if they jeopardize the satisfaction of lower level needs which are irrelevant to our growth objectives. They pile on threats—*important* threats with which we must deal—and thereby distract us from our growth.

The third criterion for selecting environments which are not too threatening involves the consequences of failure—that which transpires if we do not successfully adapt to the novelty and do a good job. Planning for *failure* is critical to the *success* of growth projects, this pattern being one of the fundamental paradoxes of growth. Remember that experimentation is one of the integral phases of our learning cycles. In order to learn and to grow we must be able to mess up as we try out different things. Environments which are too threatening do not have room for failures, whereas those which are *not* too threatening—the kind which we want—*do* have some latitude for experimentation. This criterion urges us to ask ourselves the following questions: "Are the demands of the environment such that my growth plan must be *fail-proof,* or is the environment *fail-safe?*" "Do disastrous consequences result from my failure to achieve my growth objectives immediately, or does room exist in the environment for trial and error?" "Is the experimentation phase of the learning and growth cycle appropriate in this setting?" Environments which are not too threatening are fail-safe rather than fail-proof. They work *with* the dynamics of growth—which require some failure, some experimentation—rather than *against* these natural processes. For example, the person who wants to grow in the area of group leadership should choose to chair an innocuous church committee rather than to head up a key task force at work or in a highly-visible city club. Failure is not only acceptable but necessary when integrated into the larger success of growth. Recall the advice of the saying mentioned earlier, "Good judgment is usually the result of experience. And experience is frequently the result of bad judgment" (Schlesinger, 1978, p. 555). Environments which are not too threatening accommodate this crucial process of experimentation. Without this kind of accommodation, the pressure is often too great for growth to occur.

These, then, are three criteria which can be used to select environments which are not "too threatening": (1) the environment does not surpass the one-plus-one learning threshold; (2) it does not jeopardize important needs which are irrelevant to the objectives of the growth project; and (3) it allows the project to be fail-safe rather than fail-proof. With this selection of an appropriate environment, and with the awareness of our threat patterns, we are ready for Step 3 in the process of minimizing threat in growth projects.

Step 3: Prepare for Entrance into the Environment

Patience, "a necessary ingredient of genius," Benjamin Disraeli called it (Prochnow & Prochnow, 1962, p. 203). Geniuses or not, we can use a little patience after we have identified an environment for a growth project. The tendency may be just to dive in. However, some work is still left to be done.

At least four activities can be helpful in preparing to enter the novelty of our growth project. First, based on the knowledge of our threat patterns (Step 1), we should try to anticipate as specifically as we can just what will threaten us, how we will react to it, and what will result from our reactions. Being as concrete as possible helps here. Guided imagery and simulations are two useful techniques in this enterprise. With guided imagery, we can use our imaginations in order to visualize real-life scenarios which may take place. With simulations, we also can experience anticipated futures by living out situations under controlled conditions. Each technique, which will be enhanced considerably with a skilled facilitator on hand, can feed us with rich, concrete detail regarding the interaction of our threat patterns with the anticipated novelty of our growth project.

The second preparation activity involves building supports into the environment in correspondence with the most severe of the anticipated threats (the awareness of which has been generated by the first preparation activity described above). For example, a woman who is taking a job for the first time in an organization which is dominated by male culture may discover through guided imagery or simulations that accomplishing the job's tasks does not represent a major threat. These specific responsibilties are expected to be a snap. Rather, the major threat involves working through male-female power issues which are associated with the job's relationship dimensions. In anticipation, the woman may want to build into her situation ready access to a growth facilitator who can help her to process critical incidents as they occur. This facilitator may be a counselor, friend, mentor, or ally on the job.

Whomever the facilitator may be, because of her preparatory work, the woman knows that she wants to have the support built into her environment either before entering or soon thereafter. We will have a good deal more to say about what some of these supports may be in the remaining three chapters of Part II. The important point is that the anticipated threats have corresponding supports. This provision is what helps to minimize the threat going into novelty and living through that novelty toward growth.

The third preparatory activity may sound silly, and therefore, it probably needs our attention all the more. We need to give ourselves permission to use supports when we're threatened. With male socialization emphasizing invincible autonomy, trying to go it alone may be more of a problem with men than with women. However, with some professional women trying to supplant their female sides with a male persona, rather than doing the developmentally-sound work of integrating the two, this problem may also be experienced by many women. After all, as Cynthia Scott quipped, "Successful women are asking themselves what happens now that I've become the man I always wanted to marry?" (Association for Humanistic Psychology, 1985, p. 25). Whether predominantly a male problem, or simply a human problem, self-denial of access to supports when we need them is an important issue of which all of us must be aware. For those of us who tend toward a perfectionism which tells us that we shouldn't need help...that help only burdens others, diminishes the lustre of our accomplishments, and well, if our innermost fears are to be confessed, makes us look weak to ourselves and to others...for those of us who fall prey to this type of self-defeating behavior, we might try meditating on a paradox: to be perfect, we need to accept, forgive, and work with our imperfections. If that's too gamey—I kind of like it though—come up with your own way of generating a frame of mind which values the use of supports when threatened. Otherwise, the supports will be for naught, and inevitably threat will gain the upper hand.

Now, even though we have anticipated probable threats and our responses to them, have built in corresponding supports, and have given value to using those supports when we need them, one more preparatory activity still remains. We need to rehearse all of these things together: the threat, our response, and our use of the supports. From this rehearsal comes a "detoxification" of the novelty. Sure, the novelty of the growth environment will be threatening once we get there, but less so. If we prepare carefully, we can bring the magnitude of that threat down below "toxic," or unconstructive, levels. As with anticipating the threat in the first place, guided imagery and simulations—again with skilled facilitators present if possible—are two excellent techniques for this kind of rehearsal. Occasionally, I work with groups of high-school and university students who are preparing to live and study in Mexico, and as an example of the kind of rehearsal of which I am speaking, I have observed that these students have benefited tremendously from a cultural simulation called Bafa' Bafa' (Shirts, 1977). In the simulation, two strikingly different cultures are created in about twenty minutes in two separated groups. Then, for a little over an hour, exchanges of small groups of visitors occur between the "cultures." In the processing between each visitation and at the end of the simulation, the degree to which the students have experienced many of the elements of a real-life intercultural event, including even some characteristics of culture shock, is truly stunning. Made real were the threats that they would feel, the responses that they would make, and the supports that they would use and find significant. This kind of rehearsal in preparation of growth's novelty is easy to skip, but very important not to.

So, in preparing for our novel environments, at least four activities are crucial: (1) anticipating the interaction of our threat patterns with the novel environment, (2) building supports which correspond with the most significant threats, (3) gaining permission from ourselves to use those supports, and (4) rehearsing. These procedures are the constituent parts of Step 3: preparing for entrance into the environment. Steps 1 through 3 have emphasized things which we can do to minimize threat before we are actually in the growth environment. Step 4 focuses on what we can do once we are there.

Step 4: Concentrate on Proactivity While Immersed in the Novelty

While in the fray, sometimes we find difficulty keeping our heads about us. Speaking of growth projects as battles may sound a bit melodramatic, but I think that those of you who have tried to manage everyday affairs toward some growthful end will resonate with the metaphor. For example, Maslow has remarked:

One must sometimes talk to one's graduate students in the social and psychological sciences as if they were going off to war. One must speak of bravery, of morals and ethics, of strategy and tactics. The psychological or social scientist must *fight* to bring truth about the hot subjects. (Maslow, 1966, p. 17)

In our case, the "hot subject" is growth. Keeping our heads about us in growth projects means that we somehow remain proactive... somehow oriented toward transformative change...in the midst of it all. Six tips may help us with this challenge.

First, we need to remember the general goals of our growth project. These goals are the "why" behind the predicaments in which we may find ourselves as we go through our growth project. Without a "why," we have only the predicament...which is not particularly motivating. We need the meaning provided by our goals in order to help us to endure the difficulties.

Second, we need to stick to the knitting. In our growth project, general goals have been translated into concrete objectives, which if accomplished should lead to growth. We need to concentrate on these concrete objectives and avoid a harried, thoughtless activism. This kind of focus reduces threat.

Third, we need to encourage loose-tight thinking in ourselves. We need to focus both on the general goals and on the specific objectives which will ultimately allow us to achieve these goals. We must be "tight" about preserving the order provided by this relationship between the general and the specific. However, we must be "loose" enough to adapt as well. If the specific objectives are not achieving the goals, or if the goals prove to be unrealistic or irrelevant, we must be able to make adjustments in mid-project. Proactivity is encouraged and threat is reduced as we gain confidence in our ability to retain a goal-directed order which can flex with unexpected realities.

Fourth, we need to anticipate ambiguity. All of the planning in the world will not elminate ambiguity. Uncertainty is simply a fact of life for those of us who lack omniscience. We need to see ambiguity as a lifelong companion rather than as an enemy. When it appears, we should set an extra place at the table and include it in the festivities instead of bolting the door and spoiling the evening with fearful peeking out of the window.

Fifth, we need to avoid meta-level fear. We need to acknowledge that no matter how tolerant of ambiguity and novelty we become, feeling a little uneasy in new situations is natural. We need to accept this normal response and resist being uneasy about our uneasiness. The spiral of anxiety can really take off if we give in to this meta-level intensification. I think that this kind of spiral is what Franklin Roosevelt had in mind when he told the American people in the midst of the Great Depression. "The only thing we have to fear is fear itself" (Roosevelt, 1933).

And finally, we need simply to keep going. A profound difference exists between forward-thinking persistance and backward-thinking quitting. Resting is fine. Even momentary distractions are constructive. For example, the word for having fun in Spanish, *divertirse*, literally means to divert or distract oneself. Growth goes better with fun, I think. We don't need to be Calvinistic about the whole thing. For those of us who tend to get a little too serious about our various projects, a new variation on an old locker room saying has cropped up, "When the going gets tough, the tough go shopping." However, this kind of distraction is constructive insofar as it rejuvenates us. Human beings seem to be goal-directed. When we shift to an all-embracing escapism—when escape becomes our goal, or anti-goal—things just don't seem to go well for us. We feel yucky. The recommendation to persist in our growth projects is related to an attempt to harness the power of this natural goal-directedness for the accomplishment of the specific goals and objectives of our growth project. With confidence in our ability to persevere, the threat of new situations diminishes: we become secure with the knowledge that somehow we'll make it.

In summary, these six tips can help us to remain proactive in novel situations: (1) focus on the point of putting yourself through the threat of a novel environment—the goals of the growth project, the payoff; (2) concentrate on the concrete tasks which relate to achieving the general goals, stick to the knitting; (3) exercise loose-tight thinking, have a plan but be willing to adapt it as you go along; (4) expect ambiguity and tolerate it; (5) anticipate your fear and avoid meta-level fear—being afraid of being afraid; and (6) persevere. With these forward-thinking provisions, we can better overcome threat when we encounter it face to face, and can better accomplish the kind of transformative change which we desire. A colleague of mine calls it *burning through* rather than *burning out* (R.W. Peterson, personal communication). Proactivity is good for burning through difficult situations.

We began this chapter by pointing out that growth prospers with a proper combination of challenge and support. Finding ourselves, or putting ourselves, in novel situations can provide the necessary challenges. But challenges of this type are usually threatening, and too much threat can subdue or even prohibit growth. So we must learn to minimize the threat which we introduce with our novelty. This chapter has provided some pointers on how to achieve this delicate balance between challenge and support.

In the next chapter, we will continue to develop the theme of supports—specifically, supports dealing with the learning cycle. Learning is the *sine qua non* of growth, some new knowledge or skill always being added and integrated as a fundamental part of the growth process. So, we next turn our attention to ways in which growth environments can be planned so as to be optimally supportive of each phase of the learning cycle.

CHAPTER **9**

SUPPORTIVENESS OF THE LEARNING CYCLE

The Master said, Yu, have you ever been told of the Six Sayings about the Six Degenerations? Tzu-lu replied, No, never. (The Master said) Come, then; I will tell you. Love of Goodness without love of learning degenerates into silliness. Love of wisdom without love of learning degenerates into utter lack of principle. Love of keeping promises without love of learning degenerates into villainy. Love of uprightness without love of learning degenerates into harshness. Love of courage without love of learning degenerates into turbulence. Love of courage without love of learning degenerates into mere recklessness.

Confucius, *Analects*
(Waley, 1938, pp. 211-212)

A Seventh Saying could be added: love of growth without love of learning degenerates into greeting card inscriptions...sweet-sounding, but empty, rhetoric. Learning provides the substance of growth. Without it, no growth occurs.

LEARNING'S ROLE IN GROWTH

Addition plus transformative integration—this is how we have defined growth. Knowledge or skills are added, and as they are integrated with existing knowledge and skills, transformation occurs. A new whole evolves—either of some part of ourselves or of our entire selves. Learning begins this growth process by providing the additional knowledge or skills. Without the additions resulting from learning, nothing new exists to integrate, and transformation does not occur. The system remains the same, and growth evades us.

*Learning, then, is a **necessary** ingredient of growth.* Try to think of some concrete instance of growth in which new learning was *not* being integrated. Pretty difficult, right? Learning is a necessary element of growth not just because of the way in which we have defined growth. Rather, experience teaches us of learning's necessity. Our theory is grounded in life, not the other way around.

TWO KINDS OF LEARNING

Learning may be a necessary condition of growth, but is it *sufficient?* In other words, if learning occurs, does growth necessarily follow?

In order to answer this question, we need to distinguish between two kinds of learning: simple learning and transformative learning. With simple learning, knowledge or skills are added. Period. Significant transformation of the whole is irrelevant to the concept. This kind of learning is probably that which John Pomfret had in mind when he wrote, "We live and learn, but not the wiser grow." (Pomfret, 1700). Simple learning is a necessary but *not* sufficient condition of growth.

In contrast, the other kind of learning—transformative learning—is synonymous with growth. With transformative learning, a new whole results. This type of learning is the kind which Chinese sages tied so closely to moral development. For example, Tzu-hsia wrote:

> One who studies widely and with set purpose,
> Who questions earnestly, then thinks for
> himself about what he has heard
>
> —such a one will incidentally achieve
> Goodness.

(Waley, 1938, p. 225)

And Confucius advised urgency about this kind of learning:

> Learn as if you were following someone [with] whom you could not catch
> up, as though it were someone you were frightened of losing.

(Waley, 1938, p. 136)

These teachers were concerned with the development of "Goodness," and they saw transformative learning as essential to the evolution of the person's moral perspective—necessary *and* sufficient to growth.

The apparent ambivalence to the significance of learning which we find in writers—East and West—can be understood by examining the kind of learning to which they are referring. If it is simple learning—merely piling up knowledge for its own sake—the commentator often sounds jaded and cynical about learning. If the sage is referring to transformative learning, the commentary is usually reverential and enthusiastic, almost evangelical.

One of the problems with distinguishing between simple learning and transformative learning is that life does not hold still for static categories. In other words, new knowledge or skills may be added, but knowing what the addition's role will be in future transformations may be difficult. We may wonder, "Is the addition only simple learning? Or am I in some middle stage of transformative learning?" Pigeonholing the experience is probably not particularly important, as long as our predominant value remains transformation. With a focus on growth, simple learning has a way of becoming transformative learning.

The point of this discussion of learning is to underline its significance in the growth process. If we take growth seriously, we need to become better at being our own teachers. We need to become more competent at *self-directed learning*. As we plan our various growth projects we need to try to construct environments which are supportive of our learning. So, in the remainder of this chapter, we will review the phases of our learning cycle and examine environmental elements which can facilitate the necessary learning-work at each phase.

REVIEWING THE LEARNING CYCLE

To get started, we need to refer to David Kolb's experiential learning model which was introduced in Chapter 5. Kolb has crystalized the way in which we learn—not just in the classroom, but in life—into four simple phases (Kolb, 1984). First, he says that we begin with *concrete experience*. For example, say that we are parents engaged in the ongoing learning project of understanding our children. In the beginning of these learning cycles, we simply have the daily experiencing of our children—the play, the fights, the hilarity, the torments. Next comes *reflective observation*. We recall our concrete experience with the kids and mull it over. Perhaps we do this at the end of the day when they have been put to bed. Next, we move to *abstract conceptualization*. As we are sitting in the armchair, perhaps we begin to form some generalizations about our children and what is happening in their lives right now. Then, based on these generalizations, we generate some plans for making things better for them. The next day, we try out our understanding and our plans as we move into the *active experimentation* phase of the learning cycle. Concrete experience, reflective observation, abstract conceptualization, active experimentation—round and round we go, and where we stop, I think that it's fair to say, nobody knows.

Two dimensions structure this learning cycle: (1) *abstract-concrete,* and (2) *active-reflective.* A complete learning cycle includes both ends of both poles which ideally occur in a particular sequence. Or, from a slightly different viewpoint, we can see that the learning cycle involves integrated phases of *outer-oriented* and *inner-oriented* activities. We move from outer-oriented experience to inner-oriented reflection and abstraction, then to outer-oriented experimentation. We can see that in the learning cycle an interplay exists between what could be loosely called *introversion* and *extroversion.*

Abstract-concrete, active-reflective, introverted-extroverted— the phases of the learning cycle seems to include many of the possibilities of human personality. However, although we each tend to have the capacity for these various modes, and even though we all go through each of the phases of the learning cycle, most of us have preferences for some phases over others. Each personality is unique. Each of us has our own peculiar style. Our way of learning is a part of our personality, and so the fact that each of us has our own particular learning style is not surprising. This style emerges from our differing preferences for the various phases of the learning cycle. We could perhaps find someone whose personality orientation is equally abstract and concrete, equally active and reflective, and equally introverted and extroverted. However, most of us lean one way or the other on these continua.

For example, take the situation of learning a new job. The *explorers* (concrete experiencers) will want to get right out there and mix it up, acquiring as much hands-on experience as possible with nothing in particular already in mind other than the general goal of learning the job. The *meditators* (reflective observers) will prefer to take time to muse over related, previous experiences before diving in, and then they will want plenty of opportunity to process each new experience as it occurs. The *philosophers* (abstract conceptualizers) will want to do some background study—probably including a close examination of the organization's policies and procedures manual—in order to create a conceptual framework for the new job, and then will take pleasure in continuing to refine this framework as the experience unfolds. The scientists (active experimenters) will look forward to trying out their ideas about how to start a new job, and will eagerly anticipate identifying key problems so that they can get right to trying out possible solutions.

Of course, these examples are highly stylized and over-simplify a complex situation. The discussion also simplifies Kolb's theory which allows for various combinations of these four types (in other words, preferences for more than just one phase of the learning cycle). But I hope that the point is clear: we all manifest different styles of meaning-making and skill acquisition.

How does the Kolb model help us in planning our growth projects? It does so in at least three ways. First, the model points out that each phase of the learning cycle is essential even though we may prefer some phases more than others. Second, it helps us to be aware that we will tend to neglect planning for nondominant phases of our learning cycle. For example, people with outer-oriented learning styles (preferences for concrete experience and active experimentation) will tend to neglect creating opportunities for the learning cycle's inner-oriented phases (reflective observation and abstract conceptualization). And third, the model gives us a clear framework with which to plan: four phases...four corresponding sets of supports.

ENHANCING SUPPORTIVENESS OF THE LEARNING CYCLE

Because learning is so critical to growth, our objective here is to determine ways to create environments which are supportive of the learning cycle. But what does supportive mean?

Supportiveness

In basic terms, the concept of supportiveness includes at least three ingredients. First, an environment which is supportive of a particular phase of the learning cycle provides *resources* for the central activities of that phase. Second, the environment allows *time* for the use of those resources. And third, the environment reinforces the *appropriateness* of the use of resources and time for the successful completion of the learning phase.

Concrete Experience

Let's say for example that we have worked for ten years as a counselor in an agency and that we are offered, and accept, a position as a supervisor in that same organization. Our growth project focuses on becoming a good manager. Supporting the concrete experience phase of our learning cycle is easy. We simply arrive at work each morning. "Eighty percent of success is showing up," Woody Allen quipped, and with regard to the concrete experience phase of the learning cycle, he may be right.

However, we do need to discriminate among the kinds of concrete experiences available to us and try to make sure, as much as possible, that they relate to our specific developmental goals. For example, we may want to grow into a dynamic leader, while the organization's administration may desire that we learn to be a good bureaucrat. This kind of discrepancy may require some maneuvering on our part in order to yield the type of concrete experience necessary for our particular growth project. We may need to involve ourselves in some new project in which our leadership is appropriate and necessary, rather than contenting ourselves with implementing a well-established program with a firm chain of command and a long history of how things should be done.

Reflective Observation

So there we are, immersed each day in the concrete experience of trying to be a supervisor. But to learn from this experience, we also need a time and place in which reflecting on this experience is appropriate. In busy adult life—replete with work, family, and community responsibilities—conscious planning for this reflective period is often necessary. In my classes, many participants have said that they use commuting time for this kind of rumination. Carpooling may conserve energy and diminish pollution, but I wonder what its impact has been on our learning cycles. Maybe the loss of reflection-while-commuting is for the best, since the number of traffic accidents is all too high. Who knows how many fender-benders result from people opportunistically seizing driving time for reflective observation. Catch-as-catch-can is alright for reflective observation, but planning regular opportunities is far better.

Remember that we not only need a time and place for reflection, but we also need an environment which supports the use of that time and place for this activity. This need may require us to win the cooperation of others in our growth project. For example, a couple may agree that reflecting aloud with each other on the happenings of the day is an appropriate part of the evening dinner ritual. Or, if a person finds journal writing to be an effective instrument of reflection, he or she may need to gain agreement in the home environment that spending a certain amount of time each day in sequestered writing is appropriate.

Especially helpful in gaining environmental support is creating a concrete, situational need for reflection—something which transforms reflection from a *discretionary* activity into a *necessary* activity. Job-related, continuing education can serve this role. For example, assignments may require us to relate the course's concepts to our work setting. Then, if we need them, we have a demand and therefore an excuse to reflect on our new experiences as a supervisor. This strategy of building in environmental demands for reflection is particularly useful for those of us whose learning styles, or the learning styles of our significant others, do not emphasize reflective observation. Also, it can be applied to any of the other phases of the learning cycle.

Abstract Conceptualization

Now we are having our new experiences as a supervisor; we are reflecting on them; but we must also derive some generalizations from them. The environmental needs of abstract conceptualization overlap to some extent those of the reflective phase of the learning cycle. Those of us who are good at pulling conceptual categories and principles from our experience may be able to utilize the times and places which we have established for reflection also for abstract conceptualization.

However, many of us will need additional resources for this phase. For example, hearing what other people have come up with in acquiring a meta-level, conceptual perspective on experience often provides a useful catalyst. We may need to seek out some "theorists." A variety of media for this kind of encounter are possible: printed matter, television, letters, face-to-face contacts, etc.

As with the other phases of the learning cycle, we need to plan into our growth project appropriate resources and time for this activity. For example, as a new supervisor, we may need to ask around in order to identify the best management books and then make time to read them. Once again, continuing education can provide a useful support. It can offer not only beneficial resources but also an appropriate environment in which to be more conceptual than we normally are in everyday life.

Active Experimentation

Finally, we need to plan "labs" into our growth projects. We need places to try out our conceptual understandings and their implications. We need a place where we can fail without terrible consequences. As a new supervisor who aspires to being an organizational leader, we need situations in which we can fall on our face without losing face.

Perhaps the workplace can provide us with these kinds of opportunities: for example, small projects with limited visibility and ramifications. Maybe we need to look outside of the work organization to our children's schools, our church, or our civic groups for appropriate laboratories. Simulations in management training classes may also provide useful options.

Most of us find ourselves in the position of experimenting as we go along in life, whether or not a great deal is on the line. Some situations simply demand that we act, ready or not, and we just do the best that we can with what we know, or suspect. However, we will find ourselves in this undesirable circumstance of counting on the untried much less often if we actively plan into our various growth projects appropriate time and resources for experimentation.

We began this chapter by pointing out how essential learning is to growth. And now we close by summarizing the kind of environment which is supportive of the learning cycle. Primary to learning seems to be an interplay of outer-oriented activities (concrete experience and active experimentation) and inner-oriented activities (reflective observation and abstract conceptualization). Environments which are supportive of development encourage us to reach out *and* to reach in as we pass through the learning cycle. Open exploration must be appropriate; opportunities must exist for reflecting on these explorations and formulating generalizations about them; and testing these new conceptualizations and practicing new skills must be possible. These are all environmental characteristics which we can enhance...if we plan for them. This enhancement results in an environment which promotes our growth rather than resists it.

We now have some sense of the significance of learning to our growth. We next take up something which is crucial to learning: information.

CHAPTER 10

INFORMATION RICHNESS

Obviously, a man's judgment cannot be better than the information on
which he has based it.

Arthur Hays Sulzberger (1948)

In 1976, having used the city bus system to establish a foothold
for our two careers in the Portland area, my wife and I decided that
we needed a car. Actually, we knew that we needed a car long before
that. Something about using the bus to search for an apartment,
move our possessions, and make our various job interviews at all
hours of the day and evening helped to establish the need. Walking
our eighty-pound German shepherd, who was not allowed on the
bus, the fifteen miles to our new apartment was also a clue. We
considered pretending to be blind since guide dogs were permitted
on buses, but we knew that our goofy, high-spirited dog could never
pull it off. Arriving at work all through the long, wet Oregon winter
looking like drowned rats and catching numerous colds (or maybe
just one long one) also served to impress our eco-conscious minds
that a car was necessary. What finally turned the trick was that we
could afford one. So, we went shopping.

Around this time, the discovery had been made in California—
the hearth of many fantastic innovations—that a Ford Pinto could
function quite effectively as a fire bomb if struck from the rear,
which had something to do with the gas tank being placed in just
the right spot to be punctured upon rear impact. News of this
discovery hit the media and caused quite a stir. Most people did not
like driving fire bombs. So, a large number of Pintos entered the
used-car market at very low prices. Ever vigilant for a bargain—and
very much in need of one—this phenomenon intrigued us. Perhaps
the engineering defect was not present in all of the model years, we
thought. All the years were selling cheaply because of the general
scare, but perhaps some of them were actually safe. We decided to

investigate and found that the design *had* changed and that only certain years were being recalled for repairs. So we bought one of these "safe" Pintos. Boy, were we impressed—not only with our nice little car, but also with our shrewdness. Not long after, we got our very own recall notice. Apparently, we too were the proud owners of a fire bomb.

An error had not existed in our logic. Rather, we had gotten "bad" information...or perhaps, we had gone looking for just certain information. We have all watched people do strange things. But I continue to be impressed by the fact that when I talk with the people whom I have observed behaving oddly their actions often make perfect sense, given the information with which they are working.

Just as learning is essential to growth, so too is information crucial to learning. In this chapter, we will explore the role of information in our learning and growth cycles, as well as ways in which we can enhance its richness as we go about planning our various projects.

THE PRIMACY OF EXPERIENCE

Let's start with the critical, first phase of the learning cycle: concrete experience. This is the input phase of our meaning-making. This is the time during which we acquire the raw material which our reflection and abstract conceptualization will later refine. Many writers have noted the fundamental significance of this phase of our knowing. For example, Nietzsche wrote,

> Ultimately, nobody can get more out of things, including books, than he already knows. For what one lacks access to from experience one will have no ear (Nietzsche, 1967, p. 261).

Nietzsche is not saying that we can only learn things which we already know. He does not see our personalities as closed systems which are somehow preordained at birth, or before. Rather, he is saying that we cannot conceptualize something for which no experiential base exists, even if that foundation lies only in our imagination. When we think about the sequence of the phases of the learning cycle—concrete experience, reflective observation, abstract conceptualization, active experimentation—the remark makes perfect sense. The poet John Keats made a similar observation:

> Nothing ever becomes real till it is experienced—Even a proverb is no proverb to you till your Life has illustrated it (Keats, 1951, p. 210).

The point which both Nietzsche and Keats are making is that to an important degree what comes out of our minds depends on what goes in.

But for some reason, this fact is often overlooked. We put the cart before the horse when we leap over concrete experience to emphasize abstract learning. Near the beginning of his important book, *Experience and Nature*, John Dewey made reference to the primacy of concrete experience and the tendency of philosophers who had preceded him to devalue it:

> The serious matter is that philosophies have denied that common experience is capable of developing from within itself methods which will secure direction for itself and will create inherent standards of judgment and value. .... To waste of time and energy, to disillusionment with life that attends every deviation from concrete experience must be added the tragic failure to realize the value that intelligent search could reveal and mature among the things of ordinary experience. .... The transcendental philosopher has probably done more than the professed sensualist and materialist to obscure the potentialities of daily experience for joy and self-regulation. If what is written in these pages had no other result than creating and promoting a respect for concrete human experience and its potentialities, I shall be content. (Dewey, 1958, pp. 38-39)

Whether we like it or not—whether or not our learning styles focus on concrete experience, which is probably *not* the case for scholars and other "knowledge producers" in our society—we cannot escape the fact that in the beginning, there is the experience.

Think about the implications of this fact. The kind of events which we experience has a tremendous impact on the nature of the world which we create—the way in which we see ourselves, other people, groups, organizations, societies, the environment, our gods. These events provide us with the raw material which we shape into a more or less coherent world view.

However, events do not just happen to us. We *perceive* them. We play an active role in *constructing* events. Our experience forms our world view which then filters and shapes our experience. This pattern helps to explain why such great significance is placed on the early experience of the child. Once a particular world view gets going—a world view which may or may not be constructive for the individual—it tends to reinforce itself by filtering future experience.

For example, Abraham Maslow has described two distinct modes of knowing: one which he calls *experiential,* and the other which he labels *spectator* (Maslow, 1966, pp. 45-65). In experiential knowing, the person is deeply engaged in the event; he or she is involved...engrossed. In spectator knowing, the person is detached ...watching. If we come to value one mode of knowing over the other, then we will tend to employ it in future experience. A world view which values detached knowing will tend to elaborate a world view of detachment. Similarly, a world view which values engaged knowing will be inclined to develop a world view of engagement. Of course, each approach has its advantages and disadvantages: for detachment, freedom exists, but also possible alienation; for engagement, rich relationship occurs, but also perhaps crippling enmeshment. Maslow gave what I think is good advice when he suggested that the most desirable position is to be able to employ either mode of knowing and then to use the one which is most appropriate at the time. Based on our learning theory, we can see that this would tend to produce a more complex and more highly developed world view—one which is founded on polychromatic, rather than monochromatic, experience.

The point which I am making here is really two-fold. First, the events which we experience have a crucial effect on what we learn. And second, we play a major role in construing the nature of those events. Remember that the context for these remarks about learning is our own growth. No growth occurs without learning. What I am essentially saying is that planning our growth projects we need to try to build in as many pertinent experiences as possible and we need to try to approach these experiences from as many points of view as possible (which is another way of saying that we need to be "open"). The events which we encounter, and the way in which we perceive them, provide the information of that first crucial stage of the learning cycle—concrete experience.

DEFINING INFORMATION RICHNESS

Perhaps this is a good time to explain what I mean by information "richness." The concept involves two dimensions: *quantity* and *quality*. With regard to quantity, needing richness means that we require *lots of information*. This need is a simple volume issue.

The quality dimension is a bit more sticky. At least three criteria of quality come into play here. The first criterion is the *relevance* of the information to our growth objectives. We can have a huge amount of the information, but if it is irrelevant to the objectives of our growth project, then it is of low quality.

The second criterion of quality is the *accuracy* of the information. All information has a source, and each source has its own particular frame of reference. This frame of reference shapes the information issued by the source. Of course, pure accuracy is an illusion. Nonetheless, some information is more accurate than others. We need to try to ascertain the motivation of the information source. Does it have a strong interest in our seeing the world in a certain way? In our feeling or behaving in a certain way? Are we getting description? Interpretation? Evaluation? Cross-checking of sources is an important technique in assessing the "accuracy" of information. Information about which a broad perceptual consensus exists is of higher quality than that for which little agreement is present.

Finally, the third criterion of quality is *variety*. The objective in planning for information richness is not only to get as much highly relevant, accurate information as possible, but also to acquire it from as many diverse perspectives as possible. We may have a tendency to seek out information sources whose frame of reference is like our own. But in the interest of protecting ourselves from our own biases, foraging for difference is important. For example, if we are detached and rational, then we should inquire as to how people who are engrossed and intuitive see the situation. Information pools which represent only a few perspectives are of less quality than those which incorporate many.

ENHANCING INFORMATION RICHNESS

This, then, is what is meant by information richness. In planning the concrete experience phase of our growth project, we need to keep this framework in mind, just as we should remember it in planning each successive phase. As was pointed out earlier, however, the concrete experience phase is especially important because it is the period during which we acquire the new input of life-material which we will later shape into new concepts, feelings, and behavior.

This shaping begins in the second phase of the learning cycle—reflective observation. This is the phase in which we ruminate on the information garnered from our concrete experiences. We go back over that information, explore its implications, and begin to create its meaning for us. Additional information may facilitate the work of this phase as well. For example, exploring the reflections of other people who have had similar experiences may help tremendously. Conversations, published journals, autobiographies, biographies, television programs, movies, novels, and so forth may provide good sources of this kind of "second-hand" information. The experience itself provides the "first-hand" information, but exploring what other people have made of their experiences may help us in making sense of our own.

This process of making sense of our experience continues in the third phase of the learning cycle—abstract conceptualization. In this phase, we move from exploring our experiences to trying to draw some conclusions from them. Here, we attempt to form some generalizations which can help us to understand the world better and to act more effectively. Once again, additional "second-hand" information may enhance the quality of this phase's outcomes. This is a good point to seek out other peoples' conceptual frameworks regarding similar situations. Sometimes called theory, sometimes called philosophy, theology, beliefs, opinions, or common sense...called all kinds of things, what we want are the abstract categories and principles which people have formed as they have gone about trying to make sense out of situations which are like those of our growth project. Once again, a wide variety of sources are possible: face-to-face and mediated (publications, television, movies, etc.).

With the final phase of the learning cycle—active experiment-ation—we again direct our attention toward gathering first-hand information. This time, instead of *input* as in concrete experience, we are looking for *feedback.* With active experimentation, we are trying out our new learning and growth. We are experimenting in order to see if we have "got it." Sophocles, writing in the 5th century B.C., captured the essential importance of this phase when he wrote,

> Without experiment there cannot be
> Assurance, howsoever firm thy faith

(Sophocles, 1913, p. 305)

In the active experimental phase, we need confirmation of the meaning we have made during the reflecting and conceptualizing phases of our growth. This requires information. In this phase we ask, "How are we doing?" We need feedback. Wise planning for growth means that we need to try to build in these sources of feedback. Without them, the final leg of the learning and growth cycle is weak.

In closing, we can see that information richness is an issue which has vital significance for each phase of the learning cycle. Two of the phases—concrete experience and active experiment-ation—can be called *outer-oriented* because our attention tends to be directed outward toward immediate experience in the environment. These phases are those in which we try to generate information in the form of first-hand input and feedback. The other two phases—reflective observation and abstract conceptual-ization—can be called *inner-oriented* because our attention is inclined to be focused inward upon the processing of information which has already been gathered. Additional information in the form of other peoples' processing of their own experience can also be useful here. Although information is important in each phase, it is especially crucial in the outer-oriented phases. Remember what Nietzsche observed, "For what one lacks access to from experience one will have no ear" (1967, p. 261). This fact means that in planning our growth projects we need to place special emphasis on the information possibilities of the environments which will provide the stage for our concrete experience and active experi-mentation. We need to generate specific strategies for enhancing the information richness of these environments. We must devise ways to multiply sources when they are few and amplify them when they are faint. Without this rich information, growth may not occur. But with it, we give ourselves something solid with which to work.

Next, we turn to the issue of getting help with this work, as we explore the role of learning facilitators in growth projects.

CHAPTER **11**

LEARNING FACILITATORS

It is not good that the man should be alone; I will make him an help mate....

Genesis 2:18 (King James Version)

I get by with a little help from my friends.

John Lennon and Paul McCartney,
"With a Little Help from My Friends" (1973, p. 265)

Reggie Jackson steps in at the plate, our attention riveted on him, and drives the ball so high and so far that even he stands in awe of the blast...watching the ball, which a few moments earlier raced toward him at over ninety miles an hour, now bounce off the roof of Tiger Stadium, hundreds of feet away. The home run, the Nobel Prize, the Academy Award, the Woman of the Year Award, the promotion to CEO, they focus our minds on the individual and on the achievement. Individuals and achievements, the two run together for us to become *individual achievement*. We need our heroes and heroines. They inspire us. They give us idealized models to which to aspire. But with this idealization—this making super-human—we can lose sight of the actual process of achievement. No matter how extraordinary the person—and many of our heroes and heroines are indeed extraordinary—the accomplishment is rarely, if ever, an individual achievement. The magnificent deeds arise from a long history of relationships. The same is true with our growth: we get by with a little help from our friends.

At Marylhurst, a college for adults at which I work, we have a somewhat unorthodox graduation ritual which helps to highlight the relationships behind each and every individual's remarkable achievement—the earning of a baccalaureate degree, usually after some twenty-odd years while working full-time and being a parent and partner at home. We have no visiting dignitary whose presence brings prestige to the college but whose remarks seem general and irrelevant to the graduates and their families. We have no valedictorian to spotlight. Instead, each graduate has the opportunity, if he or she chooses, to say a few words about the meaning of this accomplishment in his or her life and to thank people who have helped to make it possible. Normally, I hate graduations. But I never miss a Marylhurst commencement. Somehow, the ritual represents growth accurately to me. Each individual is honored, which is as it should be. Each person, in his or her own way, is heroic. But also, each person's relationships are honored. The individual achievement receives its proper recognition, but the networks—those wonderful relationships behind the throne— take a bow as well. This kind of statement—this blending of individual and group acknowledgement—grabs our hearts and leaves the message that something real and important has happened here. The ceremony shows us that *individual* growth is in many ways a *systemic* outcome. This is a principle of great significance, greater probably than the messages of all of the graduation dignitaries who have ever sipped their water, cleared their throats, and told their opening anecdote. This is a principle which we can use to plan our growth: we need help...we need learning facilitators.

WHAT IS A LEARNING FACILITATOR?

A learning facilitator is any agent which helps us to move productively through the learning cycle. Each phase of the learning cycle has its own distinct tasks, and learning facilitators support us as we attempt to accomplish these tasks. They help us to avoid getting stuck. Accomplishing these learning tasks—a key to growth—involves cognitive, emotional, and behavioral challenges. We need support and guidance as we decide what to think, how to feel, and what to do. Learning facilitators provide this support and guidance.

The Mentor Ideal

The ideal form of the learning facilitator is the *mentor.* In Greek myth, Mentor was the person whom Odysseus trusted most among all of the Ithacans. While Odysseus was away on what turned out to be a twenty-year ordeal, Mentor was the person to whom he commended the development of his son, Telemachus. The word mentor has come to mean a wise and loyal adviser or teacher.

Learning facilitators who are mentors are consumate growth facilitators. They understand the difference between simple learning, which elaborates a current perspective, and transformative learning, which is synonymous with growth. They understand what growth is—its addition and transformative integrations; its endings, neutral zones, and new beginnings; and its rhythms of alternating transition and stability. They understand the resistance to change within us and within our worlds. They understand our grieving as we grow out of former perspectives. They understand the courage required of us as we grow, and they affirm the courage within us to meet our inevitable challenges. They also see the limits of our courage, and they know ways to make growth easier for us. They understand the conditions within ourselves and within our worlds which promote rather than prevent growth, and they teach us about these conditions and make interventions in order to bring them about. In short, they understand the whole ball of wax when it comes to growth, plus they are on our side: they are wise, and they are loyal.

The Common Reality

If you are feeling egregiously deprived for not having had this kind of person in your life, rest assured that you are not alone. While a few people may have enjoyed a relationship with such a mentor, most of us have not. The mentor just described is an ideal type—sort of a super-human, mother/father figure...sensitive and strong, nurturing and knowing...all things which we need to help us to grow.

What most of us experience in our lives are bits and pieces of the mentor ideal. For example, a counselor may be there for us as we process the ending of an old way of life and try to focus a vision of what is to come. This new vision may involve getting a certain kind of job, whereupon a supervisor may appear who recognizes our potential, hires us, and facilitates our movement through the organization. Meanwhile, a trusted friend may be supporting us emotionally as we set down our first roots in our new life. Often, not one person, but several people, even many, each with a key contribution, help us in the overall process of our growth.

Significance of the Ideal

So, why even bring up this mentor ideal? First of all, being on the lookout for mentors never hurts. Who knows, we might even find one. One thing is certain: we need to be able to recognize a mentor when we see one. Buddhist literature is full of stories about bodhisattvas (enlightened beings) who walk the earth in unimpressive guises. Thinking about what a mentor is helps us to look beneath the surface appearance of people in order to see if we have indeed bumped into one.

Secondly, the mentor ideal provides us with a set of characteristics which we can try to incorporate into our own personalities. In many ways, we have the potential to be our own mentors. That is really what self-directed growth is all about. Essentially, this becoming our own mentors is the objective of this book. Understanding what growth is and what promotes it...this awareness is within our potential. To a certain extent, we can learn to carry our mentor within us.

Finally, given that we often receive our mentoring in bits and pieces, thinking about the mentor ideal helps us to have an image of the whole which we are trying to achieve. Even if we are not as fortunate as Telemachus and do not have our own flesh and blood Mentor, and even if we have not yet succeeded in becoming our own complete mentor, we can still put together our learning facilitators in combination with our own inner mentor—such as he or she is—in order to approximate the mentor ideal.

RESISTANCE TO GETTING HELP

Getting help sounds simple enough. Then why don't we do it more often? Maybe you do. But many people do not. Why not? One important reason often involves our attitudes toward asking for, and receiving, help. The joint issues of separation and attachment... independence and dependence...autonomy and relationship...rear their heads early in our experience and stay with us throughout our lives. Attitudes which interfere with our forming productive relationships with learning facilitators can involve either side of the coin: autonomy or relationship.

Autonomy Issues

On the autonomy side, we may feel that getting help somehow diminishes our independence, that it says to the world, and to ourselves, that we are unable to stand on our own two feet and be an adult in the likeness of the idealized images of our childhood authority figures. Of course, seeking help for life's little, and sometimes herculean, challenges can develop into pathological dependence. However, it can also be seen as a mature recognition that in large part we are the product of our relationships and that trying to manage our relational networks makes sense. Furthermore, on the autonomy side of the coin, we may feel that getting help builds up a hopelessly complex field of obligations which impinges on our free movement. *Quid pro quo*—you help me, then I owe you one and must reciprocate whenever you call in the debt. From this perspective, getting help just paints us into a corner. While "sappers"—people who take relentlessly and give little in return—are pretty irritating, we may be surprised to find that for some learning facilitators, our receiving their help is gift enough. The constructiveness of their assistance bestows value on them. It says that the person has something worthy to give. Also, should a learning facilitator ask for help in return at an impossible time, we may be delighted to learn that no hard feelings result when we can say, "I just can't right now." Moreover, should we be able to deliver that help, we create the opportunity to experience the satisfaction of being a learning facilitator ourselves—the sense that we have something of value to give others.

Relationship Issues

On the relationship side of the coin, we may feel that getting help burdens people and thereby diminishes the quality of our relationships. We may feel that it creates grounds for resentment. Wanting to avoid being a "sapper" is a healthy objective, I think. However, we must realize that the dynamics of caring require that someone (or something) exists who is cared for—in this case, us. In order for the caring act to be completed, it must be received. Asking for help focuses an opportunity for a caring act, and receiving help fulfills that act. Caring is perhaps the most deeply satisfying and constructive form which relationships can take. If you are fortunate enough to have caring people in your life, then getting help from them, and achieving a constructive outcome with that help, can be one of the greatest gifts which you can give them. Paradoxically, allowing someone to care for us can be an act of caring on our part. The interplay surrounding helping can produce a profoundly bonding rather than destructive event in human relationships (some excellent resources on the intra- and inter-personal dynamics of caring include Fromm, 1956; May, 1969; Mayeroff, 1971; and Noddings, 1984).

A Common Problem

While reading this discussion about counter-productive attitudes towards getting help, you may have been wondering what all the fuss is about. If so, feel happy. These negative attitudes *are* a problem for many people. Time and time again, I have watched individuals try to achieve growth by themselves for many of the reasons just mentioned. Saying that the problem is more often experienced by men than by women is tempting because men are socialized to be the autonomy experts, and women, the relationship experts—John Wayne on the one hand, and Mother Theresa on the other. However, as we have just seen, negative attitudes towards getting help can appear on either side of the autonomy/relationship coin. More likely, resistance to getting help is a *human* problem of which we *all* must be aware.

A SIMPLE PLANNING PRINCIPLE

So, let's assume that we have conquered any negative attitudes we may have had about getting help and that we are ready to move ahead with planning environments which will support our growth projects. The advice at this point is simple: we need to think ahead about that with which we will need help (the discussions in the first ten chapters should have generated some concrete ideas), and we need to identify agents in our growth environments which will assist us with the most critical of these items, or we need to plan these agents into our environments (incidentally, a useful resource on these networking issues is Maguire, 1983, especially the chapter called, "Networking and Self-Help," pp. 27-41).

Possible Facilitator Relationships

Relationships with learning facilitators can come in many forms. They may be relationships from our personal lives—

relationships with partners, parents, friends, relatives, or children. Or they may involve professional, role-based relationships, such as with supervisors, colleagues, teachers, trainers, consultants, ministers, or counselors. Interactions in these facilitator relationships may be face-to-face, or they may occur in mediated form, such as through correspondence and telephone conversations. Geography need not limit us. The relationships may incorporate two-way exchanges or may be one-way affairs, such as in receiving guidance from the work of a particular author, composer, artist, or film-maker.

Need for Awareness and Creativity

Once again, the important things are being aware of that with which we need help and being creative and perceptive about who can provide that help. Growth, or transformative learning, involves leaving something; it includes endings and neutral zones. We may have a special need for emotional support for this work. Growth also involves new beginnings, or adding and integrating new content or process within our personalities so as to transform them in some large or small way. We need assistance with cognitive, emotional, and behavioral issues for these challenges. Furthermore, we need help with the various tasks of each phase of the learning cycle: exploration, reflection, conceptualization, and experimentation.

With awareness of our special needs we can better plan in relevant help. For example, a student in one of my development classes—a professional woman in her forties—was shaping a growth project which focused on developing her computer competence. Included in the project was the objective of overcoming a rather sizable computer anxiety. For a variety of what seemed to me to be insightful reasons, she determined that learning in her home was better than in a classroom and that her computer-whiz husband should not be her teacher. Apparently, her computer klutziness had become a minor relationship issue. So, her husband was out of the running as a teacher, which left her with a fairly supportive environment except for one glaring deficiency— no instructor. About two days after finishing the weekend workshop covering this growth material, I walked by one of the bulletin boards at the college and saw this notice:

I NEED A TUTOR FOR ME
+ my KAYPRO II computer
(with processor).
MY OTHER NEEDS ARE:
*That you set up
an environment of
minimal threat
*That you are
supportive and
patient.

FEE??   Call _____

Being a resourceful person, she had advertised for a learning
facilitator. Also, she had anticipated her vulnerability to her
husband during the course of the growth project and had reached
an agreement with him that the subject of computers was off-limits
between them until she felt that she had successfully consolidated
her learning. So, in effect, she had also enlisted her husband as a
helper.

Another student in one of my classes taught me a useful
exercise for identifying learning facilitators not only at the
planning stage but also while in the thick of things actually
carrying out a growth project. In this exercise, participants sit in a
circle. One by one, they stand and present to the group their project
and that with which they feel they need particular help. The group
members reflect on the presentation, and if they feel that they can
contribute, they stand individually and suggest specific resources
with which they are familiar. The exercise can increase several
important items: (1) comfort in asking for help, (2) ability to phrase
projects and needs clearly, (3) concrete ideas for help, (4) sensitivity
to the unexplored resources around the person, and (5) awareness
of one particular process for discovering these resources—asking
clearly and openly. This exercise may have to be adapted for
everyday social situations. After all, our friends—many of whom
may already think that we are weird enough—might conclude that
we have gone completely over the falls if we were to gather them
together one night, sit them in a circle, present our growth project
to them, and ask them for learning resource and facilitator
suggestions. But on the other hand, who knows? Depending on the
nature of your friends, they might understand. Colleagues and
strangers probably would not be sympathetic, however. Regardless

of the situation, the exercise does seem to have elements which can translate into strategies for generating good ideas. Furthermore, it teaches us a process which is useful in both the planning and implementation phases of a growth project. We need to have foresight with regard to lining up our learning facilitators, but we also need to be persistent and perceptive in identifying them once in the growth environment.

In conclusion, we need to remember the following: that our individual growth is usually a systemic outcome as much as an individual effort, that we can enhance the likelihood of our growth by trying to make sure that our social networks include appropriate learning facilitators, that we may have attitudes towards getting help which interfere with our developing productive relationships with learning facilitators, that we need to have a keen sense of our specific tasks if we are to find appropriate help, and that we need to be ever-ready to identify a learning facilitator and to receive his or her help. Amos Bronson Alcott once wrote:

> The true teacher defends his pupils against his own personal influence. He inspires self-trust. He guides their eyes from himself to the spirit that quickens him. He will have no disciples.(Alcott, 1841)

Even if we are not fortunate enough to have such a selfless mentor, we can still be mentored—guided by an environment which we have enriched with a diverse and multi-talented cast of learning facilitators.

PART III

WHAT CAN THE PERSON CONTRIBUTE?

The constancy and pervasiveness of the operative presence of the self...is the chief reason why we give so little heed to it; it is more intimate and omnipresent in experience than the air we breathe. .... Yet till we understand operations of the self...the ultimate and important consequence is...a matter of accident.

John Dewey, *Experience and Nature*
(1958, pp. 246-247)

We arrive at this point having examined what growth is and some of the environmental conditions which promote it. But growth is a systemic outcome which relies on more than just the environment to produce it. Growth results from an *interaction* of the person and the environment. So, our exploration is not complete without investigating some of the qualities of the person which foster growth.

In Part III, we will look at five of these qualities: *self-awareness, growth motivation, learning skills, knowledge of the developmental process,* and *developmental planning.* As with the environmental discussion, we need to make two points explicit at the outset. First of all, this list is not exhaustive. You may want to add other items. The trick is to gather knowledge of as many growth experiences as possible—those of other people as well as your own—and then, to see if some features emerge as common themes in these different experiences. From this process comes a list of growth facilitators, things which we need to understand and to enhance if we wish to foster growth. My hunch is that you will find the ten environmental and personal qualities discussed in this book to be a good beginning list.

Secondly, we need to remember that these qualities are elements which *promote* growth, not *guarantee* it. Their presence increases the chances of a successful growth experience. I think that some kind of alarm should go off in our heads when someone tells us that if we just do some particular thing, success is just around the corner. That's silly, in my opinion. Growth is a complex process which we need to approach respectfully. However, respect does not mean passivity. We can play a major role in shaping the outcome of our various growth endeavors. Understanding these ten environmental and personal facilitators gives us some tools with which to do this shaping.

Objectives for Part III: To explore five features of the person which promote development, and to improve our skills at actualizing them in day-to-day living.

CHAPTER **12**

SELF-AWARENESS

"Why, he hasn't got anything on!" the whole crowd was shouting at last;
and the Emperor's flesh crept, for it seemed to him they were right. "But all
the same," he thought to himself, "I must go through with the procession."
So he held himself more proudly than before, and the lords in waiting
walked on bearing the train—the train that wasn't there at all.

Hans Christian Andersen,
"The Emperor's New Clothes" (1978, p. 59)

According to this story, many years ago an Emperor lived who
loved clothes above all else. Two swindlers learned about the
Emperor and hatched a scheme to capitalize on his obsession. One
day they arrived at court claiming that they could weave the
loveliest of fabrics and could make from this material the most
beautiful robes the kingdom had ever seen. To make the bait
irresistible—and to secure their swindle—they added that the
cloth would have a special quality which the Emperor would find
very useful. Those people who were unfit for their situation or who
were intolerably stupid would not be able to see the cloth. The
Emperor was overjoyed at the prospect of not only gaining
exquisite, new robes but also discovering the hidden incompetents
in his realm. So he hired the two swindlers and kept them supplied
with all of the gold and silk thread which they requested as they
wove his extraordinary, new garments.

One by one, the Emperor sent his trusted attendants to inspect
the progress of the exciting project. Though the weavers worked
frantically at their looms, no cloth could be seen because they
pocketed all of the gold and silk thread and only pretended to be
weaving. But the attendants did not report to the Emperor that
they hadn't seen any cloth. Fearing that they would be declared
unfit for their posts or frightfully stupid, they told the Emperor how
beautiful the material was and how pleased he would be. Figuring
that an examination of the creation was now safe—for the Emperor
also did not want to be thought incompetent—he visited the
weavers himself. The Emperor could not see anything either, but he

did not admit it. Instead, he waxed poetic about the splendor of the new fabric and commended the skill of the two craftsmen...as well he should because the two swindlers had him right where they wanted him.

Soon came the day for the unveiling, a royal procession through town. The people were enchanted with the reputation of the new robes, and everyone turned out to view them. Out walked the Emperor, proud as ever, stark naked except for his crown, scepter and slippers, with his lords behind him pretending to carry an imaginary train. The crowd gasped, which pleased the Emperor, for he thought that it indicated that his attire was a big hit. No one wanted to be thought unfit or stupid, so they all told him how lovely his new outfit was...all except for one, a child.

Not being fully socialized yet and therefore not understanding the rules of the game, the kid spilled the beans, much to the embarrassment of his father. Who wants everyone in the kingdom to know that you've got an imbecilic child?! But once said, the child's perception spread through the crowd like wildfire. Soon, the awareness which lurked in everyone's mind came out as a shout. The Emperor *was* naked!

As for the Emperor and his lords, they did the best that they could with the situation and carried on bravely as if everything was perfectly normal, but they knew that they had been fooled. What happened to the swindlers? Like so many things which fool us, they vanished from the story, and we can only speculate about their fortune.

How naked we can feel when at last we become aware. Sometimes, it can make our flesh creep, as it did the Emperor. Other times, it can bolt through us, beginning in the gut and coming out like a karate cry, as it does for some people I know. How we react depends on how embarrassed we feel. But what we find may not be embarrassing at all. We may glow like the proverbial newborn babe when we become aware of some enchanting goodness in ourselves which points towards delightful prospects. Like in a medical examination, the nakedness of self-awareness may be distressing or encouraging depending on what we find.

SIGNIFICANCE OF SELF-AWARENESS

Whether or not we like what we find, one thing is clear: high degrees of self-awareness increase the chances of growth, especially self-directed growth. Put simply, changing something is difficult when we don't know what it is or how it will react in the growth process. We cannot answer basic questions involving our growth objectives if we don't know who we are: What needs to be added to ourselves? With what in our personalities will it need to be integrated? And what will be transformed ultimately? Nor can we create resources and strategies in order to manage our environments for growth without a fair degree of self-awareness: What kind of novelty do we need? What is threatening to us? Which phases of our learning cycle are least dominant and need the most support? What kind of information do we need to balance our biases? And what kind of facilitators are best for us? Without self-awareness, we cannot tell where we need to go or how we how we should try to get there.

"Know thyself," the inscription at the Delphic Oracle instructed all who entered there. Somehow that knowledge was essential to interpreting the prophecies which were revealed at that sacred spot. Alexander Pope, writing in the 18th century, had his own version of this admonition (Pope, 1903, p. 142):

Know then thyself, presume not God to scan,
The proper study of mankind is Man.
Placed on this isthmus of a middle state,
A being darkly wise and rudely great:
With too much knowledge for the Skeptic side,
With too much weakness for the Stoic's pride,
He hangs between, in doubt to act or rest;
In doubt to deem himself a God, or Beast;
In doubt his mind or body to prefer;
Born but to die, and reas'ning but to err;
Alike in ignorance, his reason such,
Whether he thinks too little or too much;
Chaos of thought and passion, all confused;
Still by himself abused or disabused;
Created half to rise, and half to fall;
Great lord of all things, yet a prey to all;
Sole judge of truth, in endless error hurl'd;
The glory, jest, and riddle of the world!

"Riddle of the world!"...no one said that self-awareness was easy, just important. Easy or not, we need to try to increase it, and perhaps this chapter will provide some ideas on how to do that.

DEFINING SELF-AWARENESS

One of the reasons why I like the story of the Emperor's new clothes is that it highlights the two locales of the complex processes involved with self-awareness. On the one hand, we have the *intra*-personal domain. This is where the Emperor denies his own perceptions to himself. And on the other hand, we have the *inter*-personal domain. This is where the people around the Emperor do not tell him what they see (for good reason!). Self-awareness can come from either of these interrelated domains. Shortly, we will explore each arena for ways to enhance our self-awareness. But first, we need to spend a moment defining this elusive quality which we're trying to increase.

"I" and "Me"

Self-awareness can be usefully framed by using two of George Herbert Mead's concepts—the "I" and the "me" (Mead, 1962). We encountered these two tools back in Chapter 4. The "me" is self-as-object. It is what we think of when we think about ourselves. It is our self-concept. The "I" is what does the conceiving. It is self-as-subject. "I" (subject) sees "me" (object). As noted earlier, the "I" has difficulty seeing itself. As soon as the "I" focuses attention on itself, it becomes the "me." Reading this passage may be producing some confusion, and perhaps even a need for an aspirin. But the distinction being made here between these two aspects of the self is really quite simple. Taking a moment to repeat the exercise recommended earlier should bring home the point. Think about who you are. Then quickly shift to thinking about that which is thinking about who you are. Then shift again. Think about that which is thinking about that which is thinking about who you are. Get the idea? The "I" is indeed a slippery fish. We reach for it, but always come up with the "me."

Elusive as the "I" may be, however, it is the core of who we are. It is our constant self, ever constructing and interpreting our reality. The "me" comes and goes, depending on whether or not we are thinking about ourselves. But the "I" is always there. With higher levels of consciousness, learning theorist David Kolb has noted how we come to realize the core role of the "I":

> ...one's self becomes identified with the process whereby the interpretative structures of consciousness are created, rather than being identified with the structures themselves. (Kolb, 1984, p. 158)

That is, we come to experience ourselves more as the "I" which is creating the "me," rather than simply as the "me." Or put metaphorically, we come to identify ourselves with the person which is looking into the mirror, rather than with the image which we see there.

A Definition

Now comes the denouement. What does all this "I" and "me" business have to do with defining self-awareness? Quite a lot, actually. We can see that the "I" is really the most essential self. The "me" is merely a reflection of it. But we also know that perceiving the "I" directly is extraordinary. Usually, we see it in reflection as the "me." The objective of the pursuit of self-awareness is knowledge of the "I." However, all we have to work with is knowledge of the "me." Self-awareness, then, becomes the congruence between the "I" and the "me." Self-awareness is really a *congruence continuum* between these two aspects of the self. With high degrees of self-awareness, nearly perfect congruence exists between who we are and who we think we are (the "I" and the "me"). What we see is what we get. With low degrees of self-awareness, huge incongruence exists between who we are and who we think we are. In other words, what we see is what we see, but what we get is a big surprise. Most people do not like this kind of surprise, which is one reason why self-awareness is so highly valued. Certainly, in growth projects this type of surprise is to be avoided.

A FRAMEWORK FOR SELF-AWARENESS PROCESSES

So, if this is what self-awareness is, and if high degrees of it are so important, how do we go about increasing it? This is not an easy question, but I've got a few suggestions. Before discussing these ideas, however, developing a framework to organize them will prove useful. Earlier we talked about how the processes which produce self-awareness can be seen to fall within two interrelated domains: intra-personal and inter-personal. A simple scheme, called the Johari Window, has been created to express these two domains (Luft, 1969). Incidentally, exotic as it may sound, the name "Johari" does not belong to some Eastern tradition. Actually, it is a memorable shortening of the first names of the two psychologists who developed the model, Joseph Luft and Harry Ingham.

Essentially, the scheme is based on the recognition that either ourselves or other people can be the source of self-awareness. In diagram form, the model looks like this:

	Known to Self	Not Known to Self
Known to Others	OPEN	BLIND
Not Known to Others	HIDDEN	UNKNOWN

Open Quadrant

The open quadrant involves those things which I know about myself, and which other people know about me as well. For example, I cherish a good sense of humor. Used constructively, it indicates an extensive and benevolent frame of reference to me. Other people know this fact about me because even if I haven't told them already, they can easily observe it in my behavior, much to their delight or irritation, depending on how they feel about humor in general and my humor in particular. If our open quadrant is relatively large— that is, if much of what can be known about us is known by ourselves *and* by those around us—this means that we tend to disclose a lot and that we are inclined to ask for feedback from others frequently.

Hidden Quadrant

The hidden quadrant refers to those things which I know about myself but which other people don't know. For example, I know that...well, if I told you, then it wouldn't be in the hidden quadrant. All right, here's one little disclosure. I'm a fifth generation Oregonian; I drove until recently a Volkswagen micro-bus with a bed in the back; and my grandfather was a mountainman. However, despite the craze in Oregon and throughout the country for outdoor recreation, and despite appearances, I have never been backpacking. I don't even like camping. As a matter of fact, I much prefer cities to wilderness. This disclosing is fun. I may as well add that despite my interest in personal growth, I have never had a professional massage, and I have never set foot in a hot-tub. Granted these disclosures are not earthshaking, but at least they harmlessly illustrate the hidden quadrant. It encompasses things which I know about myself which other people do not. If our hidden quadrant is large—that is, of all the things that can be known about us, we know a great deal, but others know very little—it often means that we solicit a lot of information about ourselves from others, but disclose very little in return.

Blind Quadrant

The blind quadrant is an unsettling one. It involves things about us of which other people are aware but of which we are not. This is the fly-open-in-public quadrant. The phenomenon of the Emperor's new clothes would fall into this category. Also exemplifying this quadrant is the situation in which a person whom we know from years of experience to be well-intentioned but extremely judgmental comes to us and declares that he or she wants to be a counselor because of a deep love for people and a desire to help them. Our perceptions indicate that this love is attached to an idealized version of people and that normal, everyday screwballs like many of us drive the person up the wall. So we do our best to move this awareness gently from the blind quadrant over to the open quadrant in order to create the opportunity for the person to deal with it constructively. The person may not be so lucky, however, and a psycho-rapist may be lurking nearby. Being constructive is not high up on the psycho-rapists' priority list. Instead, they enjoy ravaging people with information from the blind quadrant. People with large blind quadrants frequently disclose a great deal but ask for very little feedback about themselves. Also, by necessity, they often develop a thick emotional armor to protect against attacks by roving psycho-rapists. Unfortunately, this armor also seals them off from more benevolent messengers from the blind quadrant.

Unknown Quadrant

Finally, we have the unknown quadrant—those things about ourselves of which no one is aware. The philosopher Charles Peirce once wrote of consciousness:

...our who past experience is continually in our consciousness, though most of it sunk to a great depth of dimness. I think of consciousness as a bottomless lake, whose waters seem transparent, yet into which we can clearly see but a little way. (Peirce, 1958, p. 335)

The unknown quadrant involves that knowledge of ourselves which lies beyond the limits of our ability—and that of others—to see into that lake. In Jungian psychology, the notion of the collective unconsciousness provides an example of material from the unknown quadrant. About the collective unconsciousness, Carl Jung wrote,

The great problems of life...are always related to the primordial images of the collective unconscious. These images are balancing or compensating factors that correspond to problems which life confronts us with in reality. This is no matter for astonishment, since these images are deposits of thousands of years of experience of the struggle for existence and adaptation. (Jung, 1971, pp. 220-221)

Somehow, according to Jung, we all carry within us, far beneath the surface of Peirce's lake of consciousness, the residue of generation after generation of human experience. Being unconscious to all of us, this material falls into the unknown quadrant. Personally, I don't know whether or not I buy this theory, although it definitely intrigues me. I do know, however, that each of us has facets which are as yet unknown by ourselves or others. People with large unknown quadrants are often characterized by neither disclosing a lot about themselves nor soliciting much feedback from others. They neither teach others about themselves, nor learn in return.

ENHANCING SELF-AWARENESS

So this is a quick rundown on the Johari Window. In terms of increasing self awareness, we can see that the objective is to explore the blind and unknown quadrants. When we are dealing with the blind quadrant, we are in search of things about ourselves which other people already know. In this exploration, our strategies need to be inter-personal:

OPEN ←———— BLIND
HIDDEN	UNKNOWN

With the unknown quadrant, we are after things about ourselves which nobody knows. In this case, we have a choice. We can use either intra-personal strategies:

OPEN	BLIND
HIDDEN ←———— UNKNOWN	

or inter-personal approaches:

OPEN	BLIND
HIDDEN	UNKNOWN

OPEN ←———— ∧ BLIND
HIDDEN	UNKNOWN

Now that the objectives are well framed, let's identify some of the intra-personal and inter-personal approaches to increasing self-awareness.

Intra-Personal Techniques

Sigmund Freud called dream interpretation "the royal road to...the unconscious" (Freud, 1967, p. 647), and certainly dream analysis can serve as a useful intra-personal technique for increasing self-awareness. Interpreting our dreams can be tricky. We need to be careful to avoid becoming too fervent about the perceived meaning of our dreams unless we have been properly trained, and even then, because various schools of thought exist regarding dream analysis, we should preserve a healthy caution about the certainty of our analysis. With this caveat well taken, however, we should be aware that even amateurs can gather some unmistakable clues about the inner-workings of their cognitive and emotional lives by simply paying attention to their dreams.

Another technique for increasing self-awareness which can be done in privacy involves interpreting our creative expressions. Recently, various types of therapy have sprung up in response to this idea that the person's creative processes can be used to expose deep material and to work with it: for example, art therapy, music therapy, and dance therapy. Letting ourselves loose to do something creative—just about anything—can not only feel good as we release pent up energy, but also it can reveal something to us about what we are thinking and feeling at unconscious levels. Again, as with all of these awareness-enhancement techniques, we need to bear in mind the warning about training and interpretation.

Journaling can be another means of intra-personal exploration. Regularly recording our thoughts, feelings, and behavior in a journal not only can be a creative exercise with all of the possible benefits just described, but also it can begin to reveal to us long-term patterns of which we had previously been unaware.

Spending time experiencing our bodies can also be illuminating. Often, we store emotional responses in various parts of our bodies. Body awareness can help to bring these tensions to light.

Also, various forms of meditation can be useful. We may simply wish to use meditation to achieve a deep state of openness in which we can experience whatever bubbles up. Or we may choose to utilize it to re-experience a particular situation, thus performing our own guided imagery for the purpose of gaining insight into our unconscious reactions to the event.

These techniques are just a few examples of ways in which we can explore our unknown quadrant by ourselves. You probably know of other methods as well. The general principle which underlies all of these techniques is that somehow they bring to the surface deep material about the self. Making sense out of this material is something which we may be able to do on our own. If we do need some help, however, we enter the domain of inter-personal techniques for increasing self-awareness.

Inter-Personal Techniques

Awareness-enhancement techniques which lie within inter-personal contexts can be organized into four general categories:

	THERAPEUTIC	NON-THERAPEUTIC
DYADIC		
GROUP		

Therapeutic contexts are situations whose definition hinges on our expressed need to be healed of some sort of psychological malady. Non-therapeutic contexts, of course, are situations which are defined in any other way—say, for example, our desire simply to get together informally in order to learn about ourselves and others by sharing our experiences. Dyadic contexts are those in which only two people are involved, while group contexts include more than two. Each of the four categories can be an appropriate means of enhancing our self-awareness, depending on our preferences (for example, we may feel more comfortable in dyads than in groups), and depending on our condition (we may or may not be in such a state that our ability to function is threatened). The important thing is that we choose contexts in which we can trust the constructive intent and the competence of the primary participants who are involved, especially the leader, if one exists. We don't want any psycho-rapists on board, particularly as captain.

Examples of therapeutic dyads would include, of course, sessions with counselors and therapists. Interactions with some ministers might also fall into this category. Non-therapeutic dyads might include relationships with partners, friends, relatives, and colleagues. Therapeutic groups are self-explanatory, but also might include support groups which may not be defined as group therapy yet which sometimes function in that way. Non-therapeutic groups which can increase self-awareness are well exemplified by classes and workshops which focus on the immediate application of the conceptual material to the participants' lives.

Cross-Checking

With all of these intra-personal and inter-personal techniques available for increasing self-awareness, the thought may occur to us that we can use more than one. In fact, this is desirable. A little cross-checking never hurts any inquiry, especially in this case where we are exploring such an important topic: the self.

Thinking at Two Levels

Actually, increasing self-awareness, like the enhancement of each of the ten conditions described in this book, can be seen as a growth project in itself. Our ability to increase the presence of each condition not only fosters growth, but it can be the chief objective of growth. Sure, as we have discussed in an earlier chapter, cross-checking helps in our efforts to increase self-awareness. But so does everything else which we have explored as a facilitator of our successful movement throughout growth cycles. An important and useful dimension of complexity is added to our perspective when we realize that each of these ten conditions—in this case, self-awareness—can simultaneously exist at two levels: at one level, as a part of the overall growth process...as an *agent* of growth; and at a second level, as the point of the process...as the *object* of growth. Recognizing this second level saves having to reiterate comments on the entire growth process when it comes time in each chapter to discuss how to enhance any particular growth-promoting condition. The whole growth process can be applied to developing any of its parts. We don't need to repeat this fact every time. We just need to remember it.

Next we will focus on a particular part of the self: our growth motivation. As we will see, our motivations play a significant role in shaping our realities, and whether or not we find growth opportunities in those realities depends in an important way on how much we truly *want* to grow.

CHAPTER 13

GROWTH MOTIVATION

In spite of illness, in spite even of the arch-enemy sorrow, one *can* remain alive long past the usual date of disintegration if one is unafraid of change, insatiable in intellectual curiosity, interested in big things, and happy in small ways.

> Edith Wharton, *A Backward Glance*
> (1934, p. vii)

Demand for variety is the manifestation of the fact that being alive we seek to live, until we are cowed by fear or dulled by routine. The need of life itself pushes us out into the unknown.

> John Dewey, *Art as Experience*
> (1934, pp. 168-169)

...say *No as rarely as possible*....separate oneself from anything that would make it necessary to keep saying No.

> Friedrich Nietzsche, *Ecce Homo*
> (1967, p. 252)

To a great experience one thing is essential, an experiencing nature.

> Walter Bagehot, *Literary Studies*
> (1911, p. 113)

"Fraught with growth opportunities," he wrote, "I am presently involved in a career search and find it to be a situation fraught with growth opportunities." The choice of the word "fraught" caught my eye in the student's paper. Strictly speaking, the word just means filled. But usually we use it when a situation is loaded with something unpleasant, such as hardship or danger. In a pickle, we might say, "The predicament is fraught with difficulties." But when happy, we usually don't say, "The time is fraught with joy for me." I tried to avoid reading too much into the use of this phrase. After all, the growth process has phases during which we may not be particularly sanguine about upcoming events. The student simply may have been in one of these vulnerable periods. However, I knew that whether or not growth transpires depends in an important way on the degree to which a person is actually interested in having it happen. In other words, in order to grow, *wanting* to grow helps a lot. We need to be motivated towards transformation, rather than preservation, of the status quo. So, I remained alert in the rest of the paper for the presence of this crucial growth motivation, and happily, I found it there.

WHY MOTIVATION IS SIGNIFICANT

One of the reasons why this motivation is so important is that our interests play a major role in shaping the way in which we create and interpret our realities. But before discussing how this phenomenon works conceptually, let's briefly consider a concrete example. Let's see how it looks in operation. For instance, take the tragicomic story of the compulsive gambler, an accountant who lived in New York City. Beneath the staid surface dwelled a wild risk-taker who lived for games of chance. His primary interest was to hit it big, and he was constantly on the lookout for tips and signs to aid his various gambling enterprises.

One night, he had a dream in which a giant, red "5" flashed repeatedly before his mind's eye. He couldn't shake the vision. It just kept pulsing before him...whether ominously...or auspiciously...he couldn't tell. Finally, the dream woke him up. He turned to the clock on the night table to see the time. There, in the red light of the clock's digital display, appeared 5:55 a.m. The three red 5's, all lined up, did not go unnoticed by him, but he tried not to make too much of it. The hour was still early, but because he knew that he couldn't go back to sleep, he decided to rise. He went to the bathroom to shave, and he couldn't help noticing as he picked up his razor that in the window which indicates how many blades are left, a 5 appeared. "Hmmm," he thought, with rising excitement, but still, he stayed in control.

Dressed and ready for work, he took a cab to the office. Reaching for his wallet to pay the driver, he glanced at the meter, which read...you guessed it...$5.55. The meter often read that amount, but this morning he gave the sum special significance. He went up to his office and discovered that he needed to spend the day working at a client's place—the address...Suite 555, 55 5th Avenue. Often he had chuckled over this address, but today all of those 5's didn't amuse him...they inflamed him. Working all day as best he could in his state of monumental preoccupation, the time finally came to total the client's revenues for the previous year. He pressed the button, and out before his hungry eyes, the calculator yielded a string of 5's so long that the sight made him dizzy.

Regaining himself, he knew that this was it...a sign. No doubts remained for him. Finally, after all those years of suffering losses, he had attained a state of gambler's grace, and the cosmos had given him a *sign*. This kind of gift was not to be ignored, for scorning it would offend the forces of the universe, he thought. So he headed for the track.

He took all of the cash which he had been able to gather during the day and placed $5,555 of it on the 5th horse in the 5th race to win. The odds were enormous against his horse. But to him this simply meant that he would win more money. The handicappers were clearly out of touch with the powerful forces with which he, on this special day, had achieved intimacy. Confidently, he went out through the doors to the stands where he could watch the race. Minutes later, in a state of shock, he passed back through these same doors. His horse had come in 5th.

Motivation and the Construction of Reality

Have you ever observed that when you buy a car, you begin to see that model everywhere? Our attention is selective, just like the gambler's. We notice that in which we have an interest, that which is relevant to what we are trying to do. The gambler was always trying to hit it big; it was his primary motivation. So he was always on the lookout for patterns which might constitute a tip, a lead, an inside track, which could direct a successful wager. In an important way, the motivation structured his reality, ultimately a tragic reality.

We do not just passively receive reality; we actively construct it. Remember that not only according to an examination of our own experience, but also in light of a considerable amount of empirical research (e.g., Toch & Smith, 1968; Segall, Campbell, & Herskovits, 1966) as well as philosophical inquiry (e.g., Berger & Luckmann, 1966; Heidegger, 1962; Husserl, 1962; Merleau-Ponty, 1962; Sartre, 1956; Schutz & Luckmann, 1973), the theory of "Immaculate

Perception" just doesn't hold water. Through our complex processes of perception, we play a major role in shaping our worlds. This fact has more than passing importance for us because the outcomes of our various enterprises depend in large part on the opportunities which we find in the world around us, a world which we help to create.

We human beings are goal-directed creatures...we're always up to something. And that which we're up to provides a major organizing element in this process of reality creation. The phenomenologist Alfred Schutz wrote:

> It is our interest at hand that motivates all our thinking, projecting, acting, and therewith establishes the problems to be solved by our thought and the goals to be attained by our actions. In other words, it is our interest that breaks assunder the unproblematic field of the preknown into various zones of various relevance with respect to such interest, each of them requiring a different degree of precision of knowledge. (Schutz, 1970, pp. 111-112)

That in which we are interested establishes what is relevant to us in our worlds. Relevance makes some things stand out, while it also causes other things to fade into the woodwork. Furthermore, these interests provide a cornerstone in the frame of reference which we use to interpret these things which stand out in our worlds. Meanings are not inherent in things; they are what we make them. So, in a very real sense, people with different motivations may experience quite different realities, even though they may be in the same situation.

MAINTENANCE VS. GROWTH MOTIVATION

As examples, let's consider the realities which result from two opposing motivations: maintenance and growth. In the reality which is influenced by maintenance motivation, change is the enemy...preserving the status quo is the goal. Within this perspective, when we analyze a situation, elements which bolster resistance to change land in the positive column, while those which promote change fall on the negative side. Novel situations which force us to change in order to cope are anathema. When we go to Mexico on vacation—if we ever do such a foolhardy thing—we stay in the Hilton and eat at Denny's. We focus on the familiar and ignore differences whose exploration would cause us to re-think our current perspective. We supply our social environment with other maintenance-motivated Americans and with seasoned Mexican tour guides who have learned that rocking people's perspectival boat can jeopardize a fat tip. Motivated to maintain our current frame of reference, we construct our world accordingly.

In contrast, let's say that we are motivated toward growth. For whatever reason—dysfunction of our present perspective or the desire for self-actualization—the impulse to preserve this status quo is weak. Instead, transformation is the goal. Put into the same situation as the maintenance-motivated person, the results of our analysis are just the opposite: elements which promote change are on the positive side, while features which aid and abet resistance to change are in the negative column. Novel situations which require us to change in order to adapt successfully are desirable. When we travel to Mexico, other Americans and tour guides are probably our least favorite companions. Instead, we seek out interactions with Mexicans which will confront us with cultural differences, heighten our awareness of our current conceptions, and help us to explore alternatives. Learning resources spring out at us, rather than remaining embedded in our perceptual fields. We are alert to environments which support our learning cycle. We actively seek out information which will help our growth. We recognize learning facilitators when we see them. In short, elements of change are supports rather than threats, and the world which we experience is very different from that of the maintenance-motivated person.

The difference between the realities associated with these two motivations—maintenance and growth—can be brought home if we think back to a time when we shifted from one to the other. Think of a period when initially you resisted change but later decided to try to change. Take a moment to guide your imagination back to that episode in your life and then re-experience it. Quite a difference between before and after, right?! Most people report that this simple shift in motivation transformed their worlds dramatically.

Maintenance motivation is not inherently bad, of course. After all, as the saying goes, "When a change is not necessary, it is necessary not to change." However, maintenance motivation doesn't go very well with growth. If on the surface we say that we want to grow but deep down we are really motivated toward maintenance, then we have a dysfunctional conflict. Everything which we *say* we are trying to do is at war with that which we are *really* trying to do. This sort of inner turmoil can be very confusing for us, not to mention the distressing effect our unpredictability can have on those around us. We need to seek congruence between our stated objective and our fundamental motivation. If we say that we are interested in growing, then we must truly have a growth motivation, not a maintenance motivation.

To summarize, being mobilized for maintenance versus being mobilized for transformative change makes a critical difference in the way in which we construe experience. With maintenance motivation, we are fundamentally oriented toward systemic homeostasis. Concentrating on the status quo blurs the horizon. With growth motivation, we give our attention to reaching the horizon. Development, as we have defined it earlier, is the goal. We are questing rather than fortified, open rather than closed. With growth motivation, our system of relevances are activated to promote transformation rather than to prevent it as with maintenance motivation. Again, to say that growth motivation is an important condition for development is simply to point out that in order to grow actually *wanting* to grow helps a great deal.

ENHANCING GROWTH MOTIVATION

So, growth motivation is crucial. All right, then, how do we go about enhancing it in ourselves? Three realizations and a paradox can help. Let's begin with the realizations.

Realization One: Rapid Change Won't Go Away

First, we need to recognize that change is constant and that it appears to be accelerating. Noting the constancy of change is certainly not a new observation. In the 6th century B.C., Greek philosopher Heraclitus is reported to have said, "...all things move and nothing remains still...you cannot step twice into the same stream" (Plato, 1926, p. 67). In the 17th century, the English poet Abraham Cowley wrote (1967, p. 106),

The World's a Scene of Changes, and to be
Constant, in Nature were inconstancy

Now, in the latter part of the 20th century, we add our observation of life's inexorable flux. Clearly, change has been an everpresent companion of human beings throughout history.

The accelerating rate of change, however, may be something new. Not long ago, a woman in her early forties who worked as a mid-level manager at a local high-tech firm met with me to explore a new graduate program which we were developing. During the course of the conversation, I asked her how things were going in her organization. She described a situation which has become common nowadays: declining sales and consequent over-staffing. The company took pride in never firing anyone and had implemented a clever and complicated scheme for "transitioning" superfluous employees. Those who decided to stay with the company were often re-assigned to different work groups. In response to this upheaval, higher management was bringing in consultants to help to congeal these new groups and to facilitate transition for individuals. "Some of the people seem to believe that if they can just get through this change, it will all disappear and go back to normal," she said pensively. Then, she added, "But I think that what they're trying to teach us is that we need to learn to manage change...this is the way it's going to be."

An accelerating rate of change is a hard thing to measure meaningfully, although people have tried. For one thing, establishing a basis for comparison between various historical periods is difficult. Whether or not the rate of change has steadily increased through human history is not crucial for our purposes, however. What is important here is accepting that most people agree that *right now* we are living during a period of rapid change and that this rapidity is likely to increase in upcoming years. This highly dynamic quality will probably dominate the environments which we will inhabit during our lifetimes, and it will strongly influence the coping skills which we will need in order to adapt. Maybe the friend whom I mentioned in Chapter 1 is right. Perhaps rapid change is the next big environmental stress which will cause an evolutionary shift in the human species. The high-tech firm just described provides an example in microcosm. Those employees who can adapt to rapidly changing organizational and industrial environments will survive in the company, and those who cannot, won't. Again, in the words of the woman with whom I spoke, someone who is a likely survivor, "...we need to learn to manage change...this is the way it's going to be."

Realization Two: Growth Helps
Us to Cope with Rapid Change

So, the first realization has to do with rapid change in *our environment* and the coping demands which it exerts. The second realization has to do with change *in ourselves* and our ability to meet these environmental demands. We need to recognize that growth is a type of change that increases our overall complexity, flexibility, and stability, and that these three qualities significantly improve our ability to cope with change. First, let's consider complexity. With growth, we become more of something. We add and integrate thoughts, feelings, or behaviors. Relatively undeveloped people are simple-minded compared to more highly developed people. The developed person has more from which to draw in trying to adapt to change or, preferably, to manage it.

Because more exists from which to draw, the highly developed person is very flexible. He or she can handle more situations, consider more alternatives, and be more creative than the less developed person, who is rigid by comparison. "A foolish consistency is the hobgobblin of little minds," as Ralph Waldo Emerson put it (Emerson, n.d., p. 19). Rapidly changing environments require the kind of flexibility which the highly developed person displays.

And lastly, because the highly developed person is flexible and can successfully handle a large number of new and old situations, he or she is relatively stable. In contrast, the less developed person is more volatile. Things have to be just so, or the relatively undeveloped person is thrown out of kilter. Being off-center, of course, is a disadvantage in trying to cope with rapidly changing environments, while being stable comes in very handy.

Realization Three: Growth Has
Become a Necessary Survival Skill

These first two realizations—that environmental demands require us to manage rapid change in order to cope, and that growth improves our ability to do so—when put together yield a third realization: growth is essential to our survival. *Rather than being a luxury, it is a necessity.* Whereas maintenance motivation is in conflict with environmental demands, growth motivation achieves congruence with them. Growth, which is often associated with higher-order self-actualization and sometimes impugned with snide innuendos about self-centeredness, can actually be seen to be a basic survival imperative.

In an important report commissioned by the Club of Rome (a highly respected global society), Botkin, Elmandjra, and Malitza explained this imperative for growth superbly (Botkin, Elmandjra, & Malitza, 1979). What we have termed growth, they call "innovative learning," a transformation of the person which they define as, "the type of learning that can bring change, renewal, restructuring, and problem reformation" (p. 10). They contrast innovative learning with "maintenance learning," a phenomenon which we have called change-but-no-growth:

> Maintenance learning is the acquisition of fixed outlooks, methods, and rules for dealing with known and recurring situations. It enhances our problem-solving ability for problems that are given. It is the type of learning designed to maintain an existing system or an established way of life. (p. 10)

Maintenance learning has been the norm, but they argue that environmental demands require a change:

> Traditionally, societies and individuals have adopted a pattern of continuous *maintenance learning* interrupted by short periods of innovation stimulated largely by the shock of external events. .... Even up to the present moment, humanity continues to wait for events and crises that would catalyze or impose this primitive *learning by shock.* But the global problematique introduces as least one new risk—that the shock could be fatal. (p. 10)

Growth, or innovative learning, they point out has pre-eminent survival value in this new environment:

> ...we are not discussing a metaphysical issue;...learning has become a life-and-death matter, and not only for people at the edge of subsistence. Even for those more secure in material provisions, the dictum "learn or perish" now directly confronts all societies—wealthy or poor—even though many of their individual members may still feel insulated from...harshness. Innovative learning for those who oversee the power that can annihilate the human race has become particularly indispensable. (pp. 14-15)

This international study group arrives at the same conclusion which we do: growth is not a "metaphysical issue" but instead a fundamental survival skill.

The Paradox: Growth
Facilitates Maintenance

So, these are the three realizations which were mentioned initially. Now comes the paradox. The purpose of maintenance motivation is to preserve the whole, while that of growth is to transform the whole. In a rapidly changing environment which demands greater complexity, flexibility, and stability, the way to preserve the whole is to transform it toward these ends. In this light, growth motivation and maintenance motivation begin to merge. In other words, in this kind of environment, the best way to maintain ourselves as an integrated personality is to seek growth.

Of course, this is only an apparent paradox. Maintaining the whole as an ordered entity and maintaining the particulars of the the whole are two different things. They refer to two quite separate orders of generalization. At the lower order, growth and maintenance war against each other—growth trying to transform the relationship of the parts of the whole, and maintenance trying to preserve them. However, higher-order maintenance—the preservation of the whole as an ordered entity—is actually served by growth's transformation. By transforming ourselves, we are better able to maintain ourselves.

Through deeply understanding this apparent paradox, we can enhance our growth motivation. We are motivated to achieve things which are important to us. By linking growth to survival, we connect it to something which is probably *very* important to most of us. With this kind of well-founded significance given to growth, being motivated toward achieving it becomes easy.

Of course, being motivated to grow isn't everything. We also need to have the skills to do it. Previously, we discussed the critical role which learning plays in the growth process—transformative learning and growth being virtually synonymous. In the next chapter, we will explore the constituent skills of learning and ways in which we can improve them.

CHAPTER 14

LEARNING SKILLS

'Tis not by age, but by instinct that wisdom is acquired.

Titus Maccius Plautus, *Trinummus*,
(1883, p. 18)

...the wise man is the man who in any one thing can read another....

Plotinus, *Enneads* (1952, p. 44)

A parent never wakes up the second baby just to see it smile.

Grace Williams
(Prochnow & Prochnow, 1962, p. 92)

We say that someone is wise. But what do we mean by that? The wise person somehow has the insight to make good judgments in complex circumstances, to handle new situations effectively, and to remain centered amidst the flux. Complexity, flexibility, stability...wisdom is really a high level of growth. Enough knowledge and skills have been added and integrated, enough growthful transformations have transpired, that the person has acquired the ability to understand life's predicaments deeply and to act constructively.

However, this growth does not just automatically come from experience. We have to do something with that experience. We have to make something out of it. We have to learn from it. Over two millenia ago, Plautus said, "'Tis not by age but by instinct that wisdom is acquired." Certainly, learning is one of the most central "instincts" in progressing upward through levels of growth. But we must not only be good at learning. We must also be reflective about it. We must turn the process back on itself, and *learn how to learn.* In this way we get dramatically better at learning and reap immeasurable benefits in increasing our ability to grow, even perhaps, eventually achieving some degree of wisdom.

DYNAMICS OF LEARNING

As we begin this discussion, the distinction which was made earlier between simple learning and transformative learning deserves repeating. Remember that simple learning—the kind which the Club of Rome report called "maintenance learning"—involves adding new knowledge or skills and integrating them with existing knowledge or skills, but without any significant transformation of the whole which those knowledge or skills constitute. For example, we may learn more, but we really don't see the world any differently. On the other hand, with transformative learning—"innovative learning" in the Club of Rome report—a transformation of the whole does occur with the addition and integration of new knowledge or skills. We learn more, and as a result, we see the world differently. Transformative learning is virtually identical to growth, and in this book, it is the intended application of our learning to learn.

Also, as we get started, we need to recall David Kolb's experiential learning model (Kolb, 1984). In this scheme, he attempts to summarize the way in which we make meaning out of experience—the way in which we learn. He says that we do so by completing a learning cycle which has four phases within it. Beginning with concrete experience, we next reflect on these events and form generalizations about them, concluding by testing these generalization through experimentation. At this point, you may want to refer back to Chapters 5, 9, and 10, for previous comments about the learning cycle. Now, with this model as a backdrop, I would like to introduce to you four characters who will help us to understand learning and how to enhance our ability to do it.

Ella

First comes Ella, the explorer. Her light brown hair is frosted golden and her skin colored a delicious *cafe au lait* from the sun of so many expeditions. In the lines around her bright eyes, she shows the effects of having faced the elements her whole lifetime. She speaks many languages but has no conscious grasp of their grammar, and she has an uncanny knack for understanding strangers in strange lands. Always ready for an adventure, she couldn't stand school in her youth, although certainly smart enough to have done well if only she could have applied herself.

Sitting in a lecture, her mind would drift to the thrills of new territory, whose frontier began just the other side of the classroom door. Ella would rather live stories than tell them...would rather be a lightening rod than a seismograph. And a restlessness exists in her which disturbs some people, but intoxicates others mightily.

Madelyn

Then comes Madelyn, the meditator. Voluptuous Madelyn is pear-shaped and fair-skinned from spending so much time indoors sitting in her favorite chair, a marvelous, old chestnut-colored affair, with high, worn arms, a sagging seat, and ample room for her to curl up. Her delicate hands feature long and graceful fingers on which she often wears rings with large, evocative stones—fire agates with enticing, deep-brown pools, picture jaspers with rustic stories to tell, and opals with encompassing, glittering swirls of pastel light. Her hands are wonderfully soft and smooth except for two callouses on her index and middle fingers which come from many hours of writing in her journal, something which she has done since she was a child. How she loves to sit in her chair and gaze out the open window to the sky beyond or look down into her rings...letting reflections come and go, building on each other, replacing each other...then record her observations of life in her journal. Introverted by nature, Madelyn frequently surprises people once they get to know her. They marvel at the stories she can tell...such detail, so many interesting connections...she seems to get so much out of each little event!

Felicia

Next we have Felicia, the philosopher. Her quick, brown eyes sparkle like jewels set in her spectacles' tortoise-shell frames. Light and lively, she darts about her study, a towering canyon of shelves filled with books by all the major thinkers in areas which interest her. Felicia is comely but forgetful of her appearance. Her comically mismatched clothes are often dusty with chalk from the hours which she spends at a huge blackboard in her study drawing lines among abstract symbols...creating, erasing, re-creating conceptual frameworks. Her ebullient smile erupts with an exquisite joy when at last she has solved a problem, when finally she has abstracted from the murkiness of a life experience its key elements and their interrelationships, when at last she has created a conceptual basis for understanding and prediction. Ill at ease with everyday chitchat, Felicia's company is nonetheless valued. People come to her with their problems. They go elsewhere for a hug and a dry shoulder to cry on. But they come to her when they're stuck and need some ideas. Though petite, her power amazes them as she cuts through their fog and delivers the pure and simple light of her theories.

Susan

Finally we have Susan, the scientist. Her muscles are lean and taught from much tramping in the fields. Her athletic body animates practical, loose-fitting khakis and well-worn, walking shoes. Across her back is usually strapped a canvas pack, richly provisioned with water, dates, nuts, chocolate, binoculars, pencils, and notebooks. People often see her in the woods, intent on observing something, taking notes, checking out some contention which she read or heard or thought up herself. When she notices them, she is friendly. She takes a keen interest in the world around her. But her conversation is rarely idle. She asks questions targeted at topics on which she is working, and her lovely eyes widen in anticipation of people's responses. Down-to-earth, tough-minded but with a wide, easy smile, Susan is trusted by folks. People love to ask her questions in return. They know that she never gets carried away with brainy theories. They know that her deepest bond is with the practical, everyday world. They understand that this world is her litmus test for ideas, and that given the choice between her books and her binoculars, she would choose the binoculars every time. They wonder about what this long-striding, cheerful woman has found, for they know that it will be useful.

The Group

In case you haven't guessed it already, each of these characters represents one of the phases in Kolb's learning cycle. Ella personifies the concrete experience phase; Madelyn, reflective observation; Felicia, abstract conceptualization; and Susan, active experimentation. They may seem like an unlikely confederation, but nonetheless, each of us has this cast of characters within us.

Imagine this group on an outing—a walk in the forest, let's say. Ella (concrete experience) and Susan (active experimentation) press to keep moving, Ella wanting to explore as many trails as possible and Susan desiring to make as many observations as she can so as to test the hypotheses on which she's focused. Susan thinks that Ella is completely undisciplined, but enjoys her spunk. Ella thinks that Susan is obsessively focused, but likes the fact that at least she has walking blood in her veins. Both Ella and Susan are exasperated by Madelyn (reflective observation) and Felicia (abstract conceptualization), who prefer sitting on logs to walking. Madelyn loves the dreamy quality of the light coming through the trees, and wants to savor the moment and reflect on its fullness and the memories which it provokes. Felicia finds Madelyn's lyrical descriptions mildly interesting but wonders about the next step, "What do these experiences mean?" She sets her mind on that question, and shares her thoughts with Madelyn. Sitting on the log, chatting, as Ella and Susan call for them to come on ahead, Madelyn and Felicia realize that they are allies of sorts, although neither one is completely comfortable with the other. Felicia sometimes becomes impatient with Madelyn, thinking that she never seems to make anything out of her reflections. Madelyn, on the other hand, occasionally finds Felicia's irremediable abstraction slightly annoying.

Quite a group! Imagine the dynamics which can result from the interaction of these four!? Whatever the dynamics might be, they're happening inside our heads. No wonder we feel a little strange some days. Usually, one or two of the characters are stronger than the others, and they exert leadership over the group. The nature of this leadership, for each of us, determines our learning style. Think of how we would prefer to go about learning something if Ella were our leader. Then imagine how we would spend our time with Madelyn as leader. How about Felicia? Or Susan? Remember that all four characters play a vital role in our learning. The point is simply that often one or two characters are more dominant than the others. For each of us, because we all have our own particular learning style, the dominant characters and the group dynamics will differ.

According to Kolb, an interesting thing happens with this group as we get older. The nondominant members of the group press to become stronger. This stands to reason. After all, a learning cycle is not complete—that is, we haven't really learned something— until each member of the group has contributed her particular gift.

Because learning has such great value in living, some part of us eventually realizes that Ella, Madelyn, Felicia, and Susan, all of them, need to be strong. So, we feel an urge to develop our weaker members.

Through skill development, we add power to the nondominant characters. As these changes in certain members are integrated into the group, its overall dynamic is transformed. The group becomes more capable and effective. In terms of our definition of growth, we add skills, integrate them with existing skills, and thereby, transform our overall learning ability.

For example, a great number of adults re-enter college with Felicia (abstract conceptualization) being a decidedly weak member of their learning group. Often they have piled up a vast number of interesting experiences, perhaps even have reflected on them a great deal, and have done the best they could to test Felicia's modest output, her generalizations. Basically, they re-enter college with a large number of unfinished learning cycles. They've done a lot but haven't made much sense out of it. "Experience rich but theory poor" is a phrase which educator Ellie Greenberg coined in order to describe these adult learners (Greenberg, 1980, p. 56). In the course of studying some theory, the ah-hah experiences begin to happen. With the abstractions to order the experience, the stuck learning cycles are freed to move toward completion. After working with theory a while, their Felicia becomes stronger. They are better able to formulate generalizations about their experience by themselves. And as the changes in Felicia's strength is integrated into her relationships with the other three group members, the overall group is transformed and strengthened. In other words, these adult students not only learn specific content, but also, they often experience a significant improvement in their ability to learn.

LEARNING TO LEARN

Thomas Draxe has called learning the "eye of the mind" (Prochnow & Prochnow, 1962, p. 155), and with regard to growth, having 20/20 vision in our mind's eye helps a lot. As discussed previously, learning is necessary for growth to occur; transformative learning is growth itself. In language slightly different than that of our discussion, Henry James nonetheless left little doubt about the reverence with which he held transformative learning:

> The power to guess the unseen from the seen, to trace the implication of things, to judge the whole piece by the pattern, the condition of feeling life in general so completely that you are well on your way to knowing any particular corner of it—this cluster of gifts may almost be said to constitute experience....(James, 1888, p. 389)

The outcome of transformative learning—of growth—is a perspective with well-founded and well-tested generalizations which enable us to make these kinds of judgments...to be "experienced" in this way...to be wise.

So, learning is important. How can we get better at it? The trick is to see learning as a "cluster of gifts." Learning is not just one skill, but rather, a group of skills. Re-visiting the characters from the learning group will be useful at this point. We need to ask ourselves what some of the things are which each one of them—Ella, Madelyn, Felicia, and Susan—needs to do well in order to get the most our of her central activity. If we can identify some of these skills—say, one for each character—then we will have a clear idea of some specific sub-skills on which we need to work in order to transform our overall learning ability in a positive way.

Concrete Experience

For Ella, the explorer, probably the most important skill is empathy. In order for her to get the most out of her explorations, she needs to be open to events; she needs to restrain her pre-conceived notions and participate actively in diverse realities.

Ella needs to know the difference between empathy and sympathy. With sympathy, when we walk into a room and see a person crying, the situation makes us sad and we experience our own sadness. With empathy, in contrast, we experience the other person's sadness (Wispé, 1968). The loss of a loved one is a time when we need empathy from others, but we usually receive sympathy. Typically, we never do so much bereavement counseling as when we ourselves are bereaved. The very sight of us reminds other people of their losses. They begin well enough, "How are you doing?" But very quickly they reveal their sympathetic mode, "I remember when I lost my father, I felt..." As for us, we usually feel...left out. The observation of this typical response is not meant to diminish the good intentions of people. It simply points out that the part of us which is Ella may tend to approach the world ego-centrically, or sympathetically, and that empathy is something on which we may need to work consciously in order to counter this inclination. With empathy, we try to experience the other person's thoughts, feelings, motivations, even bodily states, not our own. From the success of this endeavor, our experience is far richer—our explorations are far more productive—than before.

This important sub-skill of learning—empathy—has its own set of sub-skills. In a useful article on empathy, communication theorist Milton Bennett has identified six essential steps:

(1) Assuming difference

(2) Knowing self

(3) Suspending self

(4) Allowing guided imagination

(5) Allowing empathic experience

(6) Re-establishing self (Bennett, 1979; also see, Katz, 1963)

Each of these steps can be seen as a sub-skill of empathy. With empathic perceptions, we need to develop the ability to feel comfortable with difference rather than threatened by it. Other people really do construct their worlds differently than we do, and we need to learn to establish this as an ever-present operating principle. Otherwise, we miss the potentially enriching differences and impose our own experience on that of others. Self-awareness is crucial. We need to have the ability to know ourselves well enough that we can recognize when we are projecting our own perspective onto another person's experience. Confident in this sure-handed knowledge of the self, we need to be able to take the self out of the picture without worrying about our ability to re-implant it at the proper time. This elimination of the self can be a little spooky. However, learning to see the world in a relatively unfiltered state is vital. Of course, some filters will always be present, but by being able to "suspend the self," we momentarily supress as many filters as possible. We need to be able to focus our imagination on another person and, utilizing our relatively unfiltered perceptions as building blocks, create a facsimile of the other person's conscious-ness. Furthermore, we need to be able to throw ourselves into that facsimile mentally and to experience that imagined consciousness with the full capacity of our being—cognitively, emotionally, even physically. We need to be able to become the other person. Finally, we need to be able to come back from this adventure. We need to be able to re-establish the self—our own identity—so as to avoid drifting in states of extended empathy with the environment determining who we are from moment to moment.

Very briefly put, these are the main sub-skills of empathic perception. As we get better at these sub-skills and, by integrating them, as we get better at empathy, our ability to acquire more and higher quality information during our concrete experiences increases dramatically. As a consequence, Ella becomes a much stronger member of our learning group.

Reflective Observation

As for Madelyn, the meditator, perhaps her most critical skill could be called introspection. Her primary contribution to the learning group is to reflect on experience and to identify its significant detail. To perform these feats of introspection, three sub-skills are useful.

First comes good recall. Quite simply, being able to remember experiences vividly as we are going about trying to make sense out of them is very useful. Just what happened? What were other people doing? What were we doing? What were we trying to do? What were we thinking? And feeling? How about the others who were involved? What seemed to be motivating them? What did they appear to be thinking and feeling? We need to be able to recall the answers to these questions in as much detail as possible.

Next we have the ability to move knowledge from "tacit" states to "articulate" states. Remember that the philosopher Michael Polanyi described tacit knowledge as that silent kind which we have not yet spoken out loud in our minds, whereas articulate knowledge is the kind which we have raised to the level of verbalized consciousness (Polanyi, 1962, 1966). Articulate knowl-edge is easier to work with in trying to make sense out of experience because it is attached to symbols which can be readily manipulated in our analyses. In recalling our experiences, we need to be able to probe beneath the surface and to discover things which we know about events but haven't yet acknowledged overtly.

Finally, we come to the ability to analyze the recall of our experience in order to identify important causal linkages. To analyze something means to take it apart. We need to be able to take apart an experience in order to see what makes it tick. Madelyn needs to do more than just ask, "*What* happened?" She also must explore the question, "*Why* did it happen?"

As Madelyn gets better at these three skills—recall, deep awareness, and analysis—her introspective ability improves. And with this improvement, she is better able to make more out of experience. Her reflections are enormously richer, and she contributes much more to the learning group.

Abstract Conceptualization

Induction is probably the most important skill of Felicia, the philosopher. Her central task is to take the material provided by reflecting on concrete experience and to make generalizations about it. She must give an experience its larger meaning so as to provide a basis for handling new experiences. From the specific, she must formulate the general. In order to accomplish this induction, three sub-skills are useful.

First, we need the ability to associate. The part of us which is Felicia needs to be able to see connections among concrete experiences. The ability to identify similarities and differences among specific occurrences is vital if a pattern is to emerge. How is what happened yesterday like what transpired last year? How is it different? The answers to these kinds of questions generate crucial linkages among concrete events.

Next, we need to be creative. We must overcome our anxiety about the abstract and move up vigorously and creatively to the general level. We must put together in a novel way the associations which we have been making. We must create—not discover—a pattern which accounts for them. From this creative act comes an abstract generalization which in a simple form—perhaps even elegant—summarizes numerous concrete experiences.

Finally, we need to be logical. We need to be able to investigate the implications of adding this new generalization to our existing body of generalizations. Does the system of our theoretical knowledge—our philosophy—possess a logical integrity? Have we introduced some internal contradictions with our new generalization? Do we need to go back to our reflections and re-examine the validity of some of our generalizations? Just as critical reflection must pay heed to the integrity of the concrete experience, so must generalization be sensitive to the integrity of our abstact conceptualizations. Being able to identify abstract inconsistencies can take us back to experience in a very meaningful way.

These are three sub-skills which can improve Felicia's inductive: association, creativity, and logic. By increasing her inductive ability, we expand our capacity to make meaning out of past events. And with these generalizations—shorthand for our experience—we are better able to manage upcoming events. We have learned something. We have, that is, if the abstract conceptualizations are valid. They still need to be tried out in real action, not just tested in light of the mental reflections which generated them in the first place.

Active Experimentation

This brings us to Susan, the scientist. She is the experimenter in our learning group. Her central activity is applied research, and the task falls to her of trying out things to see if they work. In many ways, Susan must have all of the skills of the other three members of the group, as we will see shortly. However, because her context and purpose are unique among the group—she is out there in the world with the intent of testing something specific—her necessary skills have their own particular complexion. Four sub-skills aid that part of us which is Susan doing applied research.

First, we need to be good at what could be loosely called experimental design. We need to be adept at matching situations with hypotheses. Our abstract conceptualizations are our hypotheses. We need to be skilled at creating situations which will test particular generalizations, as well as be expert at opportunistically selecting appropriate generalizations for testing when situations present themselves to us. Furthermore, we need to be proficient at generating an empirical basis for the comparison of rival hypotheses by having an eye for *similar* situations in which *different* generalizations could be tried.

Next, we need to be skilled at multi-perspectival, but clearly targeted, data collection and recording. We need to be able to concentrate our perceptual abilities on any and all details of the experimental experience which might pertain to our hypotheses, or generalizations. And we need to be able to remember these data vividly.

Then, we need to be able to analyze that material quickly and with disciplined purpose. We need to be able to take it apart rapidly, sometimes on the spot, and extract its meaning with regard to the validity of our abstract principles.

And finally, we need to be able to revise those abstractions if necessary. They may only need a little tinkering rather than a complete scrapping. We may not have to go all the way back to the beginning of the learning cycle. We may only be a small revision away from a valid generalization. That revision will have to be tested, however.

Speed provides tremendous benefits to what we are calling applied research. If the re-design, data collection, analysis, and revision are done quickly enough, several cycles of testing revisions— each with an increasing degree of validity—can occur in the same experimental situation which we have created, or stumbled upon. Of course, this jerry-rigging is not the precise method which is prescribed for the scientific laboratory. But then, only a very small corner of the world is a scientific laboratory, and we need to do the best we can with complex, everyday situations which have their own momentum and which may be difficult to duplicate. Remember that one of Susan's central traits ' practicality.

In conclusion, we can see that many sub-skills constitute our learning ability. In this chapter, we have touched on a few of the more important ones. Undoubtedly, some have been left out. Or perhaps, you did not feel comfortable with the labels of those which were identified. Of course, you should feel free to re-name any of them, and to add or delete as you see fit. The point is that we need to try to identify some of the most important, constituent skills of learning so that we can focus on improving them, especially those skills in which we are weakest. As we integrate the improvements in each of these skills with our existing learning skills, we transform our overall learning ability—that is, our capacity to learn grows. And as we have discussed before, learning to learn has a tremendous payoff for our growth in all other areas.

Next, we move to the benefits to growth of having learned about the developmental process itself. As we will see, if we have this meta-level awareness of the process in which we're involved, we usually fare better than if we don't have it. In short, we are more competent growth-agents. Why this is true and how we can increase our knowledge of the developmental process is discussed in the next chapter.

CHAPTER **15**

KNOWLEDGE OF THE DEVELOPMENTAL PROCESS

Which is more important, the sun or the moon? The moon, because the sun is around when it's already light, but the moon gives us light when we really need it, when it's dark.

Anonymous

At first glance, the answer to this little riddle may seem silly. After all, the sun's energy is the main source of light on the earth. The moon merely reflects the sun's light. But still, something about the response rings true...

I remember once in my young and foolish days (which are perhaps indistinguishable from my present condition except that I'm nearly twenty years older) I decided late one night to visit a friend of mine who lived in a tent located in the far reaches of a 500-acre sheep ranch outside of Eugene, Oregon. This was the time of the Back-to-the-Earth Movement, and particularly in Eugene, having friends who resided in tents and tepees was not unusual. The scene sounds odd, I know—all of these middle-class folks exploring the noble savagery of their Rouseauvian roots, sitting around tribal campfires, sharing oral histories, creating and transmitting a "counter" culture...and the sniffles. At the time, however, these kinds of activities seemed like important social experiments to many people.

Anyway, this particular tent was situated in a lovely oak grove alongside a sheep trail which wound its way through the thicket. The trail was part of a maze of paths which allowed the woolly creatures to get from one pasture to another. Actually, the setting of the little, canvas abode was gorgeous—pitched right in the heart of a rugged, steep-sided valley, with dark, fir-covered slopes as

Ch 15   Knowledge of the Development Process   169

backdrops and a snow-fed river with resident great, blue herons nearby. It *was* somewhat remote, however. In order to get to it, you had to drive through two pastures—at each fence, getting out of the car to open the gate, getting back in to drive through, getting back out to close the gate, then getting back in to proceed, all the while being careful to avoid encounters with sheep. After parking the car at the edge of the last pasture, you had to walk a plank over a small creek and follow the sheep trail through the dense forest to find my friend's front "door" (or front flap to be more exact).

For some reason, having performed this feat numerous times in broad daylight, the endeavor seemed easy enough to me, even though my watch read midnight. "Piece o' cake!" I thought. "What the heck...even if it gets crazy, that'll just make things interesting." Exploring new situations was just as important to me then as it is now, although I hope that my judgment has improved regarding the likely outcomes of prospective adventures.

This night, I decided to give it a whirl. I performed all of the maneuvers necessary to arrive at the edge of the oak grove, even successfully tightroping the old board bridging the tiny creek which served as a moat. Inflated with a sense of supreme competence, I set out into the night to follow the trail. The forest was pitch black, and about five steps into the thicket I realized that—good night vision or no—seeing trail was not an option. So I took off my shoes and socks in order to feel the trail with my bare feet. That procedure having failed, I got down on my hands and knees and used my finger tips to try to identify the trail. Still no luck. "I know!" I thought, "Forget the trail. Who needs it anyway. Just walk straight to the tent, instead of winding around. Why follow sheep?! I know where the tent is...more or less." This strategy sent me crashing through the underbrush in what seemed like a straight line for the tent. I walked and walked, stumbled actually. "Too far, this is too far," I said to myself. "Turn around and try to walk a straight line to it from this side." Too far again. So I turned around and tried the straight-line strategy once more. After several additional passes, a thought occurred to me. This thought was not a hypothesis. Rather, it was a firm conclusion: I was lost...not a little lost...I was *utterly* lost. And with that realization, a reeling vertigo set in. Chaos was my context; I had no orientation whatsoever.

One shred of hope remained in my mind. "Get out of the darkness. Get out of the forest. Forget the tent. Forget your car. Just get out of the forest." The grove was a vast island of trees among the pastures. I knew that it had to end somewhere. So I just randomly picked a direction and kept stumbling ahead as straight as I could stumble with a nearly overwhelming case of confusion.

Then, suddenly, the blackness...the forest...the confusion... ended. I was in a pasture—a wide-open, enormous field of hay, waist-high, made bright by the luminous moon, a big, full moon. I could see again. "There are the mountains. There is the shape of the valley. Eugene is this way. The Cascades, that way. All right, now I know where I am." Thanks to that full moon, I could see again, and eventually found my way out of the predicament. The moon became very important to me that night.

Foolish as it may sound, something exists in the answer to the riddle at the beginning of this chapter which resonates with our experience, even if we haven't literally had to rely on the moon to find our way. No doubt, each of us has experienced those dark moments of the heart and mind when no light existed except for the pale illumination of some moon-like understanding arising from a distant horizon within us—some thought, some conceptualization, some generalization *abstracted* from our many experiences, which shed light on the concrete situation before us and helped us to make our way through it.

WHY KNOW THE PROCESS?

One of the reasons why knowledge of the developmental process is so helpful in promoting growth is that it helps us to get un-stuck. The other reason is that it helps us to keep from getting stuck in the first place. With regard to growth, this kind of knowledge benefits both our immediate problem-solving and our long-range planning.

For example, take neutral zones. Say that our old way of thinking, feeling, and doing—our old way of being—is no longer working very well and feels as if it is coming to an end. A transformation appears to be underway, but the growthful outcome is nowhere is sight. A new, integrated self may emerge, but we feel as if an even chance exists that it won't...that we have traded a somewhat troubled, dysfunctional self for one of spacy disorientation. The specter of disintegration darkens our world. When an ending occurs, we have a tendency to see the next thing which comes along as the new beginning. However, if we examine the developmental process carefully, we learn that a neutral zone sits between endings and new beginnings. We learn that most people experience this eerie interstitial space while passing through transitions, and that the phase serves very important purposes—for example, the exploration of previously deemed "exotic" ways of being. This knowledge of the transition sequence—endings, neutral zone, and new beginnings—provides us with a conceptual understanding of what we are experiencing. It gives us some moonlight on a dark night. With this abstracted knowledge, we can see a context for the neutral zone's chaos which we are currently experiencing. This knowledge helps us to avoid destructive spirals of anxiety. We are bound to feel a little anxious in the neutral zone, but if we begin to feel anxious about feeling anxious, then off we go into a dangerous spiral. Also, this knowledge helps us to keep on task. In the neutral zone, we should explore alternatives and begin to resolve an image of the new beginning. Being worried about being worried distracts us from this task and slows down the process. And finally, knowledge of this developmental sequence helps us to plan. If we know about these three phases in advance, then we can build them into our lives time and environmental supports for each of them.

I hope that the point is clear. If we have a well-founded conceptual framework for the developmental process—an empirically-based theory, if you will—then we can better understand and manage our situation at any particular point in the process, as well as better plan in advance for our productive progression through that process. We could use any of the concepts developed in this book as examples, but the point would be the same in each case. In order to be a proficient growth-agent, having a well-founded theory of growth helps a great deal. Again, Kurt Lewin's remark comes to mind, "...there is nothing so practical as a good theory" (Lewin, 1951, p. 169).

The use of the word theory might introduce some confusion here. I am not talking about abstract speculation which is disconnected from experience. Essentially I am referring to the results of our completed learning cycles—our very own experimentally-tested abstract conceptualizations regarding the nature of growth. Having a theory of growth does not mean memorizing someone else's—say, that of some famous theorist. As we discussed earlier, published theory—such as this book, for example—can be useful in the abstract conceptualization phase of our learning cycle. It can provide verbal form to generalizations which are emerging from the reflection on our concrete experiences. However, if the theory does not have some basis in our experience, it doesn't stick. We tend to abandon it in application and instead go with what we know—abstract conceptualizations which *are* rooted in our experience.

GROWTH PROJECTS ABOUT GROWTH

The upshot of this tendency to use what *we* know is simple. If we want to be good at facilitating growth, we need to place it high up on our growth agenda. We need to accomplish growth projects about growth itself.

Actually, this feat can be done quite economically. With every growth event—no matter what the topic, whether planned or unplanned—we add to our experiential base regarding the growth process. This fact means that whatever the objective of a growth endeavor—increasing computer skills, changing self-concept, improving empathy—the potential exists for a growth project about growth. Each project can really be two at once. We need to get into the habit of taking advantage of this potential. We need to have two learning cycles going simultaneously: one focused on the objective of the growth project, and the other focused on the process of achieving that objective. From this kind of bi-level growth, we not only develop specific parts of ourselves, but we also develop our meta-level knowledge of the growth process.

RESISTANCE TO LEARNING ABOUT GROWTH

The advantages of this strategy seem compelling enough. But why do some of us resist doing it? No doubt, many reasons exist. However, I would like to address one in particular. It has something to do with magic.

For many of us, the growth process is magical. We don't really understand how it works. It just seems to happen every so often.

While we would like to understand it, we are afraid that if we go poking around in our inner processes we may lose the magic. This fear is not ungrounded, we feel. For example, we may have once set out to improve our backhand in tennis. Although it was pathetic at the beginning of the growth project, we could still occasionally hit a solid cross-court shot. However, after studying the elements of a good backhand and dutifully attending to performing them all correctly, we found that we could almost never hit a decent return. We felt awkward, self-conscious, and mechanical. Or for instance, say that we once decided to improve our listening skills. We took a class in active listening, and afterwards tried to put into practice all of the elements which were advised. We felt funny, and people began to ask why we were "glaring" at them, when we thought that we were simply establishing good "eye contact." From these kinds of experiences, we conclude that reflexive consciousness spoils the magic. And with regard to something as precious as growth, it is to be avoided at all costs. We begin to break into a cold sweat at even the thought of forming abstract conceptualizations about our own process. Specific reflections about concrete events is all right, but abstractions make us very nervous.

LEVELS OF KNOWING AND DOING

What we overlook is that the feeling of mechanical self-consciousness just described is merely a phase. The magic comes back. As a matter of fact, the magic is even stronger after we have added our conceptual understanding to it. Let me try to explain why.

Tacit and Articulate Knowledge

To begin, recall Michael Polanyi's two types of knowing which we discussed earlier: tacit and articulate knowledge (Polanyi, 1962, 1966). Tacit knowledge is the silent, intuitive type. It refers to things which we "just know" but haven't said out loud in our minds. It is the domain of magic in which we have a "feeling" for how things work and what to do, for when things are right and when they aren't, but we really can't explain our feeling. On the other hand, articulate knowledge is the verbal, rational type. It refers to things which we can talk about and explain in some kind of coherent fashion. It is the domain of abstract conceptual-izations. Our very own personally-derived articulate knowledge—

those principles which are abstracted from our concrete experience—provides us with the moons which light up our dark nights when things aren't working on their own. With these two types of knowledge as a backdrop, we can identify three different levels of knowing and competence (see following figure).

Articulate Knowing
* Verbal
* Rational

Tacit Knowing
* Silent
* Intuitive

Level 1: Pre-Formal
* Naive behavioral competence—"natural" talent.
* We cannot explain what we are doing or why it works, but we can do it.
* When things don't work, we feel lost.

Level 2: Formal
* Conceptual competence.
* We can explain what we are doing and why we are doing it (we have a "theory"), although doing it may feel mechanical.
* When things don't work and we feel lost, we have a conceptual "map" to consult.

Level 3: Meta-Formal
* Behavioral and conceptual mastery.
* Through practice, we do the effective thing without having to think about it.
* When we don't have our "stuff," we can resort to Level 2.

Levels of knowing and competence.

Pre-Formal Level: Behavioral
Competence, Conceptual Innocence

In Level 1, or the Pre-Formal Level, our knowledge is predominantly tacit. We may have a basic behavioral competence, but we have no idea why the things which we do actually work. For example, as an educational counselor at a college for adults, I meet a large number of people who are coming back to school in order to obtain training and credentials for a career in human services, usually in counseling. They frequently tell me that for some reason people have always come to them with their problems and that somehow they have been able to help. They just seem to be "natural" counselors. I believe this to be an accurate self-assessment in most cases. If the psychologist Howard Gardner is right, many different kinds of intelligence exist, rather than just one (Gardner, 1983). These people may be gifted in what Gardner calls the "personal intelligences"—intra-personal, "access to one's own feeling life," and inter-personal, "the ability to notice and make distinctions among other individuals" (Gardner, 1983, p. 239). While they may be gifted in this intelligence, their talent is often raw and undeveloped, like a child prodigy in music who has never taken lessons. I ask them if they often feel stuck with someone's problem, or if they sometimes goof up by following their intuitions. They usually respond with a relieved admission and add that one of the main reasons for their returning to school is to get the "big picture" for their helping activities—that is, a conceptual framework for counseling.

Formal Level: Conceptual Competence,
Behavioral Awkwardness

This focus on conceptual frameworks brings us to Level 2 of knowing and competence, the Formal Level. At this stage, the emphasis is on articulate knowledge, and the objective is conceptual competence, in contrast to the Pre-Formal Level's naive behavioral competence. We learn to stand back from our experience and behavior and to explain what we are doing and why we are doing it in terms of a coherent theoretical perspective. For example, as the "natural" counselors just mentioned study various issues of individual psychology, social environments, and intervention methods, they develop a conscious, articulate framework for their counseling activities. From examining the various theories, they select concepts and systems which help to name and structure the tacit knowledge which has emerged from their experience. They acquire the conceptual tools to analyze personalities, groups, and communication patterns, and to guide their interventions. One of the unpleasant outcomes of gaining this conceptual competence may be the feeling that we are losing some of our "natural" behavioral competence. For example, a student who believed that she was highly empathic felt that she was losing some of her abilities by trying to take apart the empathic process in her studies. This experience is essentially the same as that of the person who feels that he or she is losing the ability to hit a backhand by trying to learn how to do it better. Studying our own process can make us feel self-conscious, and following the guidance of our conceptual frameworks can produce an awkward, "mechanical" sensation. We feel as if we are *attending to* ourselves rather than *attending from* ourselves, as Michael Polanyi would put it. However, with much practice, this feeling goes away as we move to the next level of knowing and competence.

Meta-Formal Level: Behavioral and Conceptual Mastery

In Level 3, the Meta-Formal Level, we add to our conceptual mastery that "natural" behavioral competence which we had formerly. Once again, we can do things well without thinking about it. This is a characteristic which the Meta-Formal shares with the Pre-Formal. However, two key differences exist between the two levels.

First, at the Meta-Formal Level, we can do *more* than at the Pre-Formal Level. By practicing the *new* skills which our conceptual frameworks articulate, eventually we achieve a mindlessness about them, and we add them to our repertoire of "natural" behaviors. We did not possess these skills before we studied the topic conceptually. For example, the person who believed that she was empathic discovered during her study of the subject that she was really sympathetic—that is, she felt her own feelings rather than the other person's. She was sensitive and loving, and felt her feelings strongly, which explained why she had thought that she was empathic—depth of well-intentioned feeling often being mistaken for empathy. By practicing the sub-skills of empathy, mechanically at first, she got better at empathy, and eventually achieved a state in which it felt natural. At the Meta-Formal level, she had more helping skills than she did at the Pre-Formal Level.

The second important difference between Levels 1 and 3 is that the Meta-Formal Level combines conceptual *and* behavioral competence, whereas the Pre-Formal has only behavioral competence. This means that at the Meta-Formal level of competence we have something on which to fall back if things aren't working. We have our own supply of luminous moons—our conceptual frameworks—to guide us in the dark. For example, once I was watching a baseball game on television, and the play-by-play announcer remarked that the pitcher didn't have his "stuff" that day. If you're a pitcher, having your stuff means that your fast ball is like greased lightning, that your curve ball breaks as if it's falling off of a table, and that you're "unconscious out there"—everything is going perfectly, and then some, all by itself. Then, the color announcer, himself a former pitching star, said something which caught my attention. He said that most pitchers, even the good ones, don't have their stuff more than half the time but that the good ones know how to do well even when they don't have their stuff. Doing well when we don't have our stuff...that strikes me as important, because if you're like me, we probably don't have our stuff more than half the time, just like the big-league pitchers. At the Pre-Formal Level when things aren't going well on their own—when we're stuck—we have nothing on which to fall back. At the Meta-Formal Level, in the same situation, we can resort to our conceptual frameworks for behavioral guidance. Our performance may not be inspired and natural, but at least it will be adequately competent.

Meta-Meta Levels . . .

We can see from this scheme that a productive interplay exists between tacit and articulate knowing, between mindlessness and mindfulness. This interplay can extend through many cycles. What is presently a Meta-Formal Level can become a Pre-Formal Level for a later, more highly competent, more conceptually sophisticated Meta-Formal Level. We cut off the cycles of mastery when we avoid abstract conceptualization. With regard to growth, we impede the improvement of our abilities as growth-agents when we evade reflecting on the growth process and formulating our own theory of growth.

From this discussion, we can see that not only do we need to have good learning skills as was pointed out in the last chapter, but also we need to use those skills to learn about growth itself. In the next chapter, we shift our attention from a general knowledge of the developmental process to the specific application of that knowledge. This progression brings us to the topic of planning and its role in facilitating growth.

CHAPTER **16**

DEVELOPMENTAL PLANNING

The person or the nation that has a date with destiny goes somewhere, though not usually to the address on the label. The individual or the nation which has no sense of direction in time, no sense of a clear future ahead is likely to be vacillating, uncertain in behavior, and to have a poor chance of surviving.

Kenneth Boulding, *The Image* (1956, p. 125)

A dying people tolerates the present, rejects the future, and finds its satisfactions in past greatness and half-remembered glory.

John Steinbeck, *America and Americans* (1966, p. 143)

...That man is right who has allied himself most closely with the future.

Henrik Ibsen, "Letter to Georg Brandes" (1905, p. 350)

Living in the latter part of the 20th century means having a constant and unwelcome companion—the potential for nuclear annihilation. Obviously, this fact has tended to transform attitudes toward the future. Before the bomb, for better or worse, people were able to look forward to a continuance of the human race and human civilizations. This continuity seemed secure for so many generations into the future that it was out of consciousness for most people, a "zero-order belief" in psychological language. Now, the specter of nuclear holocaust can bring a constant, although usually submerged, sense of jeopardy to our individual and collective beings. In recent years, analysts have explored the social, psychological, and spiritual impacts of living with this kind of threat (e.g., Lifton, 1979; Macy, 1983). Not surprisingly, they have found that we tend to avoid the painful stimulus and try to repress our profound fear and sadness over the possibility. If we are not careful, however, we can develop a generalized *future-phobia*—a condition in which we uncontrollably evade thinking seriously about the future.

Another factor which contributes to the inducement of this phobia is the spectacularly rapid rate of change at all scales within an increasingly complicated global system. The interconnections are so complex and the systemic adjustments are so frequent that projecting possible futures can seem like an overwhelming task. We can feel powerless. Future-phobia also feeds on this kind of intimidation.

These are just two factors which are afoot in our common social environment: the bomb and complex, rapid change. Of course, each of us has forces arising from our individual biographies which also can contribute to an aversion to thinking about the future. If we do have a touch of future-phobia as a result of these environmental or idiosyncratic forces, no matter how justified, it can create some problems for us.

NEED FOR CONNECTION WITH THE FUTURE

Ironically, evading the future only makes grim futures more likely. With evasion, we relinquish our power to influence upcoming events. After all, the future is not *necessarily* going to be terrible, and what we do today, whether we like it or not, will have an effect on tomorrow. Also, healthy human beings are goal-directed; we naturally participate in shaping the future. Future-phobia goes against our goal-directed grain and extracts a mighty psychic cost. Of course, as we have seen, the threat *is* strong, and the milieu *is* complexly dynamic. A genuine basis exists for our concern over the future. However, for the two reasons just noted—evasion gives away our power to shape the future consciously and it causes a psychologically crippling repression—future-phobia is not a constructive response to our time. In Steinbeck's phrase from the beginning of the chapter, it characterizes a "dying people," or as Bob Dylan put it, "He not busy being born is busy dying" (Dylan, 1974, p. 57).

Instead, what is needed is what Ibsen described as a state of being "allied...most closely with the future" (Ibsen, 1905, p. 350). We need to have a well-founded image of a positive future, and we need to have our present activities clearly linked to the achievement of that future. What we do today needs to be connected overtly to producing a desirable tomorrow. This kind of connection not only makes the desirable future more likely, but also it gives constructive meaning to our daily affairs. It improves both the present and the future. The *connection* to which I am referring here—the *link* between desirable futures and present activities—is *planning.*

We live in a time in which a great urgency for planning exists, in which many advocates for planning are present, and in which a part of us may feel phobically resistant to planning. However, if we do experience this resistance, we must overcome it. Planning is one of the chief tools of proactive individuals—people who accept their undeniable roles in change processes and who actively use their power toward achieving desirable futures. As I hope is clear by now, proactivity not only helps to produce a present which is made more satisfying by being meaningfully connected to desirable futures, but also it increases the chance of achieving those futures. If we wish to be proactive, and if the future in which we are interested involves growth of some sort, then we must focus on improving a fundamental skill of this kind of proactivity—developmental planning.

ELEMENTS OF PLANNING

But what are the basic elements of planning? Just what do we need to do well? In response to these questions, we will look at five planning elements and discuss them within the context of growth projects (additional resources on planning developmental projects include Breen & Whitaker, 1983; Knowles, 1975).

Objective Setting

The first planning element is *objective setting.* We need to be able to frame the objectives of our growth project clearly. Becoming scattered is so easy in a busy life. However, having clear objectives helps us to stay on task. It provides the cornerstone of our growth project's frame of reference. It gives us our organizing principle.

Objective setting is made much easier with a clear definition of growth, something which we have now. Let's say that we agree with the definition of growth which has been presented in this book. According to that framework, growth involves a transformation—large or small, process or content—which arises from integrating additional cognitive, emotional, or behavioral elements with those which already exist within us. Addition plus transformative integration, this is growth. Therefore, as we are setting our objectives for a growth project, we need to pinpoint that which we are hoping to transform, that which will need to be added, and that with which the additions will need to be integrated.

For example, in one of my classes, a woman about thirty who had resumed her undergraduate education a year earlier decided to focus a growth project on getting better at the re-entry transition. Things still weren't going smoothly for her. Although she was firmly resolved that earning a baccalaureate degree was "right" for her, for she had deep professional yearnings to practice cancer counseling because of her own experience with the disease, she had a family and was still experiencing some guilt about the time which she devoted to her studies. After much discussion, her general objective became clear. She needed to transform her self-concept. The guilt was arising from a disparity between her behavior and her core concept of herself. She needed to add to her self-concept the role of student (later, this role would be replaced by that of professional counselor). This new role needed to be integrated with her existing roles of wife and mother. So as to avoid the Superwoman syndrome—simply adding major roles to the point of burnout—she recognized that her objectives would also include transforming her conception of the roles of wife and mother. She needed to increase her knowledge of evolving models of these social roles and how these models have arisen in legitimate response to changing social conditions. She needed to integrate this knowledge of new models with her own existing models so as to transform her conceptions of wife and mother into forms which worked for her, given her current situation and her own particular biography. From ambiguity came clarity. Her objectives were lucid and compelling, and this clarity alone, even without achieving the objectives, had a soothing effect.

The objective setting phase of planning—*like each of its phases*—involves ethical considerations. Using the systems concepts which were developed earlier, we need to explore the possible ripple effects of our objectives in advance of achieving them. We may reconsider, or revise, our objectives depending on what we find. Or we may not. The decision is a matter of personal ethics. But the exploration should occur, and *some* decision should be made. That's a statement of my ethics anyway. I think that growth-agents, and change-agents in general, have a special responsibility not to be reckless.

Returning to our example, once the woman had her objectives clarified, she could see immediately that her achievement of those objectives would have an impact on her relationships with her husband and her child as well as on the overall system which the three of them constituted—their family. Incidentally, these ripple effects would occur in virtually any growth project which involved a major personality element of any member of a family. As we saw earlier, *personal* growth is in many ways a *group* affair. She thought about these impacts carefully and decided not to revise her growth objectives. In her heart of hearts, she knew that she was committed to her husband, her child, and the family, but also she knew that she was unhappy in a life consumed with wifedom and motherhood. In her wisdom, she realized that if she did not respond to her calling as a counselor this unhappiness would grow and she might begin to act destructively in her family. She might even go nuts, and then where would they all be? The transformation was important enough to her that it could not be denied. Something had to give. She felt that responding to her inner calling in a relatively controlled growth project in which her husband's and her child's needs could be carefully incorporated was far better than the possible alternative—a wild episode in which she finally snapped. Potentially, the family itself would grow and become more lastingly vital. Besides, even if it didn't, even if a divorce ensued, that would still be more constructive for all involved than the effects of having her go crazy. She was clear that the present situation simply could not continue.

The exploration of ripple effects in the objective setting phase of planning has the dual benefits of making us more caring to others and more committed to our project. By considering the consequences of our transformations, we do not begin growth projects naively. We know that our changes will impact other people. Therefore, not only do we become more sensitive to incorporating the changes within our personality systems into our various social systems, but also we do not undertake major growth projects lightly. The objectives must be very important to us, as we saw in the example of the woman going back to college. Of course, for minor growth projects, such as improving our backhand in tennis, the ripple effects are relatively insignificant, although even there, we may end up losing a tennis partner to our improved game. However, for major growth projects, the ripple effects are often monumentally significant. Deepening our commitment to the growth project by anticipating ripple effects and resolving difficult value conflicts in advance helps us to pass through the trying moments in the project. We have a solid, well-considered basis for what we are trying to do—a goal structure which is connected to our core values and which transcends mere impulsive, ego-centric gratification. With this provision, finishing what we start is easier, as well as doing so in a fashion which is as constructive as possible for all involved.

Resource Identification

The second element of planning which we will consider is *resource identification.* Once we have clarified the objectives of our growth project, we need to explore ourselves and our worlds for resources—actual *and* potential—which can help us to achieve those objectives. For example, what novel situations—the kind which would require us to achieve our objectives in order to adapt—are available to us, or could be made available if we made the effort to create them? Knowing our threat patterns, what kinds of supports to minimize threat could be incorporated into the growth project? Likewise, what are the possible supports for each phase of the learning cycle? What are the pertinent information sources? Who could be present to help us through the phases of our learning and growth? A similar survey should be conducted with regard to our internal resources. How will our self-awareness be enhanced and incorporated? What are the resources for sharpening and retaining our growth motivation? What are our strengths with regard to our learning skills? Is our knowledge of the developmental process a resource? If not, how can we strengthen it?

Strategy Formation

While resource identification involves developing lists of possibilities, the third planning element—*strategy formation*—requires us to create images of anticipated actualities. For example, in the resource identification stage, we think of as many novel situations as possible which would help us to achieve our objectives. In the strategy formation stage, we select one (or sometimes more), and make concrete plans to become involved in it. Strategy formation is the time when we get specific about what we actually plan to do. Like the objective setting phase, considering the ethical consequences of ripple effects is particularly important in strategy formation.

Determining Evaluation Methods

The fourth planning element is *evaluation*. This element requires us to think about how we will know when we have made progress toward achieving our objectives. For example, the woman mentioned earlier set her sights on integrating the primary role of student (and later professional) with her existing roles of wife and mother. She felt that she would have made progress toward this objective when she could participate in her education without feeling debilitating guilt. She also had the objective of incorporating her personal growth into her family system. On this count, she determined that she would have advanced toward her objective if her husband and her child were to report an adequate level of comfort and satisfaction with family life as she went about her studies. Of course, the two objectives and indicators of success are strongly intertwined, but you get the idea behind the evaluation task. We need to establish some way of knowing how we're doing.

Some people think that evaluation needs to have a behavioral base. That is, indication of the achievement of objectives must be tied to clearly observable things which we or other people do. But I don't go along with this entirely. While we may not always be altogether honest with ourselves, many of our growth projects involve transformations of complex internal states for which identifying simple behavioral indicators is difficult. Out of necessity, we may have to rely on self-reports of these internal states. This fact does not mean, however, that we should not try to protect ourselves from our own delusions of grandeur by gathering feedback from a variety of sources besides ourselves. For example, in addition to looking for behavioral indicators, we may want to incorporate other peoples' perceptions of our progress into our evaluation plan. To me, including our own self-perceptions as a part of the evaluation process is certainly desirable. As many social scientists have noted, trying to be perfectly "objective" in determining whether or not we have been successful can often limit us to trivial goals.

Framing Time Lines

The final planning element is *framing time lines*. This phase simply involves sequencing the various activities of the plan and attaching some dates to them. Of course, life is complex, and time lines may change many times during the course of a project. Being a stickler for punctuality is generally not helpful in a growth project. For example, the movement from one activity to another may depend on achieving a certain comfort level with the first activity. How are we supposed to know in advance when that necessary comfort level will develop? We do know, however, that rushing things is counter-productive. Or, say that we run across an especially useful source of information regarding our growth project, one which we did not anticipate. Only a foolish prospector would walk by a gold mine just because it wasn't on the map. Of course, fidelity should be to growth, not to the time line. We *should* explore that unanticipated information source for all that it's worth. Time lines simply help us to keep moving. They work against stagnation. They also encourage us to think ahead about the most productive way in which to sequence the various activities of our growth project. This attention to the interrelationships of our activities in time is by far the most important contribution of time lines, much more significant than the mere assignment of calendar dates to our tasks. A time line should be viewed as a facilitator of organization, not as a basis for evaluation. Even if we have a tendency to be hard on ourselves, we should not become upset because we achieve a precious growth objective six months behind the original schedule.

Objective setting, resource identification, strategy formation, evaluation determination, and time line framing—these are five crucial elements in the planning process. By excelling at these activities, we can create effective growth plans—those critical links between desired futures and our concrete present.

As we close this discussion, I would like to emphasize that planning is most effective when it is viewed and practiced as a dynamic process. In the first century B.C., Publilius Syrus wrote, "It is a bad plan that admits of no modification" (Syrus, 1856, p. 45). I think that we can safely say that this insight remains valid two millenia later. If anything, the principle is even more important to remember today with the increasing complexity of the world's interrelated systems. Having a clear developmental plan does not mean that the plan will not change as we implement it. We need to bear in mind that optimal planning is not something which we do once at the beginning of a project, breathe a sigh of relief, and then retreat permanently from the drawing board. Connecting desired futures to the present should be an ongoing endeavor...actually, a way of being.

CHAPTER **17**

CLOSURE

> When we have used our thought to its utmost and have thrown into the moving unbalanced balance of things our puny strength, we know that though the universe slay us still may we trust, for our lot is one with whatever is good in existence. We know that such thought and effort is one condition of the coming into existence of the better. As far as we are concerned it is the only condition, for it alone is in our power.
>
> John Dewey, *Experience and Nature* (1958, p. 420)

Each of us is an agent of change—a part of processes which day after day transform the future into the present. We have a role to play in shaping this thing which, for want of a better word, we call life—not only the collective life of the global society, but bringing the focus home, our own lives as unique individuals.

PLAYING AN ACTIVE ROLE

Our personal style of using this power lies somewhere on a continuum between two poles: *passive* and *active*. In a passive stance, the power to influence events is abdicated, and we are victims. In the active mode, we embrace our power, and we are, in the language of the day, proactive change-agents. In this book, I have advocated an active style. That is, I have recommended that we become students of change processes, that we explore the possibilities and limitations of our participation in these processes, and that we formulate clear strategies for connecting our desired futures with our daily activities.

Influence Not Control

The kind of proactivity advised here is certainly not without its humility. Reinhold Niebuhr's well-known "Serenity Prayer" comes to mind:

> O God, give us serenity to accept what cannot be changed, courage to change what should be changed, and wisdom to distinguish the one from the other (Brown, 1975, p. 3).

In just these few words, Niebuhr has captured the tension between limitation and possibility which confronts the proactive change-agent. I would be sorely disappointed if my advocacy of proactivity were to be associated with a kind of narcissistic willfulness. I do not believe that we can *make* our lives whatever we want them to be. However, I do think that we can *influence* the nature of our lives.

Burdens

Proactivity is not without its burdens. For one thing, proactivity carries with it the tension between limitation and possibility which was just mentioned. As a proactive change-agent, we must try constantly to distinguish between our legitimate limitations and possibilities. This task is not easy. In a passive mode, we focus primarily on our limitations—a far easier but less satisfying course.

Another burden of proactivity is the ethical responsibility concomitant with trying to influence change processes. In my view, the use of power should always be accompanied by a thorough ethical consideration of its consequences. Proactive change-agents, in embracing their power to influence events, also engage this responsibility. However, I would add that the decision to abdicate our power to influence events also has its ethical overtones. In other words, whether we are active or passive, we cannot escape our ethical responsibilities. In the passive mode, the issues tend to focus on the ethics of omission, whereas in the active mode, they are inclined to involve the ethics of commission. Of course, errors of omission are much easier to hide, and to hide from, than errors of commission. So, the proactive change-agent does seem to carry a more public burden with regard to ethics.

Rewards

Despite these burdens, however, proactivity has its deep satisfactions. That we are participants in change processes...that we have the power to influence change...these premises seem irrefutable. With proactivity, not only are we more likely to achieve the futures which we desire, but also, we have the satisfaction of knowing, even if we fail, that we have accepted the responsibility of our power and are doing everything within that power to make the world a better place. When each day is connected in a proactive perspective to a desirable future, it has greater significance than if it focuses merely on passive survival. Living as if we can make a difference in the outcomes of the world encourages a self-concept which departs dramatically from that which emerges from living as if we can make no difference. The purpose of our lives is enlarged and emboldened as a result of proactivity. Passive, we are haunted by the abdication of our power. Active, we know that we are doing everything we can do to make things better. And who knows, we may actually succeed.

REFRAMING LUCK

Succeeding at change is partly a matter of luck. However, I do not mean luck as it is normally construed—the chance happening of events. Taking a systems view of change processes, we see that we do play some role, large or small, in what happens to us. Two anonymous sayings capture this insight beautifully, one with which the book began:

Luck is a crossroad where preparation and opportunity meet.

The other is the one which I introduce here at the book's close:

Luck prefers the prepared mind.

These sayings, with their simple yet elegant wisdom, challenge the conventional notion of luck—a much more passive version than that proffered by these aphorisms. In these sayings...and in this book...preparation is a key theme. We must prepare for our "luck." We must understand change processes and make provisions for the outcomes which we desire.

The kind of change on which this book has focused is growth. The intent of the book has been to clarify what growth is, to explore conditions in the environment and in the person which encourage growth, and to investigate ways to enhance the presence of these conditions in everyday life. These ideas and frameworks have been meant to provide us with tools of preparation for creating our own luck, at least with regard to growth.

DON'T TAKE MY WORD FOR IT

In the preceding discussions, I have shared with you conceptual fruits from many sources—my own experience, the experiences of a large number of adults in transition, and the findings of
scholars in the field. However, if these ideas do not resonate with
your experience, I have no illusion that they will stick. If you
disagree with any part of these frameworks, the exploration of
these areas of disagreement will give clearer form to your own
frameworks. Remember that this book is a resource in *your*
learning cycle.

Facilitating growth is very much an art. But artists are not
without their guiding concepts or images. I have offered to you
these conceptual frameworks with the sincerest respect for the
creative mystery of growth. With that same respect, I encourage you
to elucidate your own. The outcome of this endeavor, I believe, will
be to enhance your success at something very dear—the art of
growing. Good "luck"!

REFERENCES

Alcott, A.B. (1841). Orphic sayings, LXXX: Teacher. *The Dial, 1*(3), 357.

Andersen, H.C. (1978). *Favourite tales of Hans Anderson* (M.R. James, Trans.). London: Faber Fanfares.

Aslanian, C.B., & Brickell, H.M. (1980). *Americans in transition: Life changes as reasons for adult learning.* New York: College Entrance Examination Board.

Association for Humanistic Psychology (1985, March). *AHP Perspective,* p. 25.

Auden, W.H. (1965). Prologue: The birth of architecture. In *About the house* (pp. 3-4). New York: Random House.

Bagehot, W. (1911). Shakespeare—The man. In E. Rhys (Ed.), *Bagehot's literary studies, Vol. 1* (pp. 112-153). London: J. M. Dent & Sons.

Bagehot, W. (1873). *Physics and politics.* New York: Appleton-Century.

Bateson, G. (1979). *Mind and nature: A necessary unity.* Toronto: Bantam Books.

Bennett, M.J. (1979). Overcoming the golden rule: Sympathy and empathy. In D. Nimmo (Ed.), *Communication yearbook 3 of the International Communication Association* (pp. 407-422). New Brunswick, NJ: Transaction Books.

Berger, P.L., & Luckmann, T. (1966). *The social construction of reality: A treatise in the sociology of knowledge.* Garden City, NY: Anchor Books.

Boswell, J. (1980). *Life of Johnson* (R.W. Chapman, Ed.). Oxford: Oxford University Press.

Botkin, J.W., Elmandjra, M., & Malitza, M. (1979). *No limits to learning: Bridging the human gap.* Oxford: Pergamon Press.

Boulding, K.E. (1956). *The image: Knowledge in life and society.* Ann Arbor: University of Michigan Press.

Breen, P., & Whitaker, U. (1983). *Bridging the gap: A learner's guide to transferable skills.* San Francisco: The Learning Center.

Bridges, W. (1980). *Transitions: Making sense of life's changes.* Reading, MA: Addison-Wesley.

Brookfield, S.F. (1986). *Understanding and facilitating adult learning.* San Francisco: Jossey-Bass.

Brown, R.M. (1975). Reinhold Niebuhr: A study in humanity and humility. In N. Scott (Ed.), *The legacy of Reinhold Niebuhr* (pp. 1-7). Chicago: University of Chicago Press.

Buber, M. (1970). *I and thou* (W. Kaufmann, Trans.). New York: Charles Scribner's Sons.

Chickering, A.W., & Associates (1981). *The modern American college: Responding to the new realities of diverse students and a changing society.* San Francisco: Jossey-Bass.

Chodorow, N. (1978). *The reproduction of mothering: Psychoanalysis and the sociology of gender.* Berkeley: University of California Press.

Cowley, A. (1967). Inconstancy. In A.B. Grosart (Ed.), *The complete works in verse and prose of Abraham Cowley, Vol. 1* (p. 106). New York: AMS Press.

Cross, K.P. (1981). *Adults as learners: Increasing participation and facilitating learning.* San Francisco: Jossey-Bass.

Daloz, L.A. (1986). *Effective teaching and mentoring: Realizing the transformational power of adult learning experiences.* San Francisco: Jossey-Bass.

Dewey, J. (1934). *Art as experience.* New York: Capricorn Books.

Dewey, J. (1944). *Democracy and education: An introduction to the philosophy of education.* New York: The Free Press.

Dewey, J. (1958). *Experience and nature* (2nd ed.). New York: Dover.

Donne, J. (1959). *Devotions upon emergent occasions & death's duet.* Ann Arbor, MI: Ann Arbor Paperbacks.

Dylan, B. (1974). It's all right, Ma (I'm only bleeding). In *before the fall* (pp. 56-59). New York: Warner.

Emerson, R.W. (n.d.). Self-Reliance. In *Essays of Ralph Waldo Emerson* (pp. 15-31). New York: A.S. Barnes.

Erikson, E.H. (Ed.). (1978). *Adulthood.* New York: W.W. Norton.

Fitzgerald, F.S. (1945). *The crack-up* (E. Wilson, Ed.). New York: New Directions.

Fowler, J.W. (1981). *Stages of faith: The psychology of human development and the quest for meaning.* San Francisco: Harper & Row.

Frankl, V.E. (1963). *Man's search for meaning: An introduction to logotherapy* (rev. ed.) (I. Lasch, Trans., Part 1). New York: Pocket Books.

Freud, S. (1967). *The interpretation of dreams* (J. Strachey, Trans. & Ed.). New York: Discuss Books.

Fromm, E. (1956). *The art of loving.* New York: Bantam Books.

Fuller, R.B. (1973). What I am trying to do. In V.J. Danilov (Ed.), *The design science of R. Buckminster Fuller* (p. 5). Chicago: Museum of Science and Industry.

Gardner, H. (1983). *Frames of mind: The theory of multiple intelligences.* New York: Basic Books.

Gilligan, C. (1982). *In a different voice: Psychological theory and women's development.* Cambridge, MA: Harvard University Press.

Goffman, E. (1974). *Frame analysis: An essay on the organization of experience.* New York: Harper Colophon Books.

Gould, R.L. (1978). *Transformations: Growth and change in adult life.* New York: Touchstone Books.

Greenberg, E.M. (1980). The University Without Walls (UWW) Program at Loretto Heights College: Individualization for adults. In E.M. Greenberg, K.M. O'Donnell, & W.H. Bergquist (Eds.), Educating learners of all ages (pp. 47-61). *New Directions for Higher Education, 29.*

Gutmann, D.L. (1968). Aging among the highland Maya: A comparative study. In B.L. Neugarten (Ed.), *Middle age and aging: A reader in social psychology* (pp. 444-452). Chicago: University of Chicago Press. (Adapted from *Journal of Personality and Social Psychology,* 1967, 7[1]).

Havighurst, R.J. (1972). *Developmental tasks and education* (3rd ed.). New York: Longman.

Heath, D.H. (1977). *Maturity and competence: A transcultural view.* New York: Gardner Press.

Heidegger, M. (1962). *Being and time* (J. Macquarrie & E. Robinson, Trans.). New York: Harper & Row. (Original work published 1927).

Hofmann, M. (1983, February 14). Changes. *The New Yorker,* p. 94.

Husserl, E. (1962). *Ideas: General introduction to pure phenomenology* (W.R.B. Gibson, Trans.). New York: Collier Books. (Original work published 1913)

Ibsen, H. (1905). Letter to Georg Brandes, January 3, 1882. In M. Morrison (Trans. & Ed.), *The correspondence of Henrik Ibsen* (pp. 349-351). New York: Haskell House.

James, H. (1888). *Partial portraits.* London: Macmillan.

Jung, C.G. (1933). *Modern man in search of a soul.* (W.S. Dell & C.F. Baynes, Trans.). New York: Harcourt, Brace & World.

Jung, C.G. (1971). Psychological types. *The collected works of C.G. Jung, Vol. 6,* (W. McGuire et al., Eds., R.F.C. Hull, Trans.). Princeton, NJ: Princeton University Press.

Kanter, R.M. (1977). *Men and women of the corporation.* New York: Basic Books.

Kanter, R.M. (1983). *The change masters: Innovations for productivity in the American corporation.* New York: Simon and Schuster.

Karr, A. (1849, January). *Les guêpes; Les femmes, 6* (304).

Katz, R. (1963). *Empathy: Its nature and uses.* London: Free Press of Glencoe.

Keats, J. (1951). *The selected letters of John Keats* (L. Trilling, Ed.). New York: Farrar, Straus, and Young.

Kegan, R. (1982). *The evolving self: Problem and process in human development.* Cambridge, MA: Harvard University Press.

Keller, G. (1983). *Academic strategy: The management revolution in American higher education.* Baltimore: Johns Hopkins University Press.

Kesey, K. (1962). *One flew over the cuckoo's nest.* New York: Signet.

Kidd, J.R. (1973). *How adults learn* (rev. ed.). Chicago: Follett.

Knefelkamp, L.L., Widick, C., & Parker, C.A. (Eds.). (1978). Applying new developmental findings. *New Directions for Student Services, 4.*

Knowles, M.S. (1975). *Self-directed learning: A guide for learners and teachers.* Chicago: Association Press.

Knowles, M.S. (1980). *The modern practice of adult education: From pedagogy to andragogy* (rev. ed.). Chicago: Association Press.

Knowles, M.S., & Associates (1984). *Andragogy in action: Applying modern principles of adult learning.* San Francisco: Jossey-Bass.

Knox, A.B. (1977). *Adult development and learning: A handbook on individual growth and competence in the adult years for education and the helping professions.* San Francisco: Jossey-Bass.

Knox, A.B. (1986). *Helping adults learn: A guide to planning, implementing, and conducting programs.* San Francisco: Jossey-Bass.

Kohlberg, L. (1969). Stage and sequence: The cognitive-developmental approach to socialization. In D. Goslin (Ed.), *Handbook of socialization: Theory and research* (pp. 347-480). Chicago: Rand McNally.

Kohlberg, L. (1973). Continuities in childhood and adult moral development revisited. In P. Baltes & K.W. Schaie (Eds.), *Life-span developmental psychology: Personality and socialization* (pp. 179-240). New York: Academic Press.

Kohlberg, L., Levine, C., & Hewer, A. (1983). *Moral stages: A current formulation and a response to critics.* Basel, Switzerland: Karger.

Kolb, D.A. (1984). *Experiential learning: Experience as the source of learning and development.* Englewood Cliffs, NJ: Prentice-Hall.

Kuhn, T.S. (1970). *The structure of scientific revolutions* (2nd ed.). Chicago: University of Chicago Press.

Laszlo, E. (1972a). *Introduction to systems philosophy: Toward a new paradigm of contemporary thought.* New York: Harper Torchbooks.

Laszlo, E. (1972b). *The systems view of the world: The natural philosophy of the new developments in the sciences.* New York: George Braziller.

Lennon, J., & McCartney, P. (1973). With a little help from my friends. In M. Okum (Ed.), *Great songs of Lennon & McCartney* (pp. 264-268). New York: Quadrangle.

Levinson, D.J., Darrow, C.N., Klein, E.B., Levinson, M.H., & McKee, B. (1978). *The seasons of a man's life.* New York: Ballantine.

Lewin, K. (1951). *Field theory in social science: Selected theoretical papers* (D. Cartwright, Ed.). New York: Harper Torchbooks.

Lifton, R.J. (1979). *The broken connection: On death and the continuity of life.* New York: Basic Books.

Loevinger, J., & Blasi, A. (1976). *Ego development: Conceptions and theories.* San Francisco: Jossey-Bass.

Lowenthal, M.F., Thurnher, M., & Chiriboga, D. (1975). *Four stages of life: A comparative study of women and men facing transitions.* San Francisco: Jossey-Bass.

Luft, J. (1969). *Of human interaction.* Palo Alto, CA: Mayfield.

Macy, J.R. (1983). *Despair and personal power in the nuclear age.* Philadelphia: New Society.

Maguire, L. (1983). *Understanding social networks.* Beverly Hills: Sage.

Maslow, A.H. (1966). *The psychology of science: A reconnaissance.* South Bend, IN: Gateway Editions.

Maslow, A.H. (1987). *Motivation and personality* (3rd ed., revised by R. Frager, J. Fadiman, C. McReynolds, & R. Cox). New York: Harper & Row.

May, R. (1969). *Love & will.* New York: W.W. Norton.

Mayeroff, M. (1971). *On caring.* New York: Harper & Row.

McGuigan, D.G. (Ed.). (1980). *Women's lives: New theory, research & policy.* Ann Arbor: University of Michigan Center for Continuing Education of Women.

Mead, G.H. (1962). Mind, self, & society: From the standpoint of a social behaviorist. *Works of George Herbert Mead, Vol. 1.* (C.W. Morris , Ed.). Chicago: University of Chicago Press.

Merleau-Ponty, M. (1962). *Phenomenology of perception* (C. Smith, Trans.). London: Routledge & Kegan Paul. (Original work published 1945).

Neugarten, B.L. (Ed.). (1968). *Middle age and aging: A reader in social psychology.* Chicago: University of Chicago Press.

Neugarten, B.L., & Gutmann, D.L. (1968). Age-sex roles and personality in middle age: A thematic apperception study. In B.L. Neugarten (Ed.), *Middle age and aging: A reader in social psychology* (pp. 58-71). Chicago: University of Chicago Press. (Abridged from *Psychological Monographs,* 1958, 72, [17, whole no. 470])

Nietzsche, F.W. (1967). Eccehomo (W. Kaufmann, Trans.) In W. Kaufmann (Ed.), *On the genealology of morals and ecce homo* (pp. 199-344). New York: Vintage Books. (*Ecce homo* originally published 1908)

Noddings, N. (1984). *Caring: A feminine approach to ethics & moral education.* Berkeley: University of California Press.

Pascale, R.T., & Athos, A.G. (1981). *The art of Japanese management: Applications for American executives.* New York: Warner Books.

Peirce, C.S. (1958). Science and philosophy. *Collected papers of Charles Sanders Peirce,* Vo. 7, (A. Burks, Ed.). Cambridge, MA: Harvard University Press.

Perry, W.G., Jr. (1970). *Forms of intellectual and ethical development in the college years: A scheme.* New York: Holt, Rinehart and Winston.

Piaget, J., & Inhelder, B. (1969). *The psychology of the child* (H. Weaver, Trans.). New York: Basic Books. (Original work published 1966).

Plato (1926). Cratylus. In H.N. Fowler (Trans.), *Plato: Cratylus, Parmenides, Greater Hippias, Lesser Hippias* (pp. 1-191). Cambridge, MA: Harvard University Press.

Plautus Titus Maccius. (1883). *The trinummus* (A.H. Evans, Trans.). Cambridge: J. Hall & Sons.

Plotinus. (1952). *The six enneads* (S. Mackenna & B.S. Page, Trans.). Chicago: Encylcopaedia Britannica

Polanyi, M. (1962). *Personal knowledge: Towards a post-critical philosophy.* Chicago: University of Chicago Press.

Polanyi, M. (1966). *The tacit dimension.* Garden City, NY: Anchor Books.

Pomfret, J. (1700). *Reason.* London: J. Nutt.

Pope, A. (1903). An essay on man. In H. Boynton (Ed.), *The complete poetical works of Alexander Pope* (pp. 137-155). Boston: Houghton Mifflin.

Porter, E. (1985). *Strength deployment inventory* (rev. ed.). Pacific Palisades, CA: Personal Strengths Publishing.

Porter, E. (1977). *Strength deployment inventory manual of administration and intepretation* (rev. ed.). Pacific Palisades, CA: Personal Strengths Publishing.

Prochnow, H.V., & Prochnow, H.V., Jr. (1962). *A dictionary of wit, wisdom, & satire.* New York: Popular Library.

Reps, P. (Ed.). (1957). *Zen flesh, Zen bones.* Middlesex, England: Penguin Books.

Roosevelt, F.D. (1933, March 4). First inaugural address.

Sanford, N. (1966). *Self and society: Social change and individual development.* New York: Atherton Press.

Sartre, J.P. (1956). *Being and nothingness: A phenomenological essay on ontology* (H.E. Barnes, Trans.). New York: Pocket Books. (Original work published 1943).

Schein, E.H. (1985). *Organizational culture and leadership: A dynamic view.* San Francisco: Jossey-Bass.

Schlesinger, A., Jr. (1978). *Robert Kennedy and his times, Vol. 1.* Boston: Houghton Mifflin.

Schlossberg, N.K. (1984). *Counseling adults in transitions: Linking practice with theory.* New York Springer.

Schutz, A. (1970). *Alfred Schutz on phenomenology and social relations: Selected writings* (H.R. Wagner, Ed.). Chicago: University of Chicago Press.

Schutz, A., & Luckmann, T. (1973). *The structures of the life-world* (R.M. Zaner & H.T. Engelhardt, Jr., Trans.). Evanston, IL: Northwestern University Press.

Segall, M.H., Campbell, D.T., & Herskovits, M.J. (1966). *The influence of culture on visual perception: An advanced study in psychology and anthropology.* Indianapolis, IN: Bobbs-Merrill.

Shakespeare, W. (1961). Hamlet. In H. Craig (Ed.), *The complete works of Shakespeare* (pp. 903-43). Glenview, IL: Scott, Foresman and Company.

Shirts, R.G. (1977). *Bafa' bafa', A cross culture simulation: Director's guide.* Del Mar, CA: Simile II.

Smelser, N.J., & Erickson, E.H. (Eds.) (1980). *Themes of work and love in adulthood.* Cambridge, MA: Harvard University Press.

Sophocles (1913). Trachiniae. In F. Storr (Ed. & Trans.), *Sophocles, Vol. 2* (pp. 253-359). Cambridge, MA: Harvard University Press.

Steinbeck, J. (1966). *America and Americans*. New York: Viking Press.

Sulzberger, A.H. (1948, August 30). Address to the New York State Publishers Association.

Syrus, Publilius (1856). *The moral sayings of Publilius Syrus, A Roman slave*. (D. Lyman, Jr., Trans.). Cleveland, OH: L.E. Barnard & Co.

Tennyson, A., Lord (1899a). The daydream. In *The poetic and dramatic works of Alfred Lord Tennyson* (pp. 128-33). Boston: Houghton Mifflin.

Tennyson, A., Lord (1899b). The princess; A medley. In *The poetic and dramatic works of Alfred Lord Tennyson* (pp. 154-216). Boston: Houghton Mifflin.

Tennyson, A., Lord (1899c). Will Waterproof's lyrical monologue. In *The poetic and dramatic works of Alfred Lord Tennyson* (pp. 137-141). Boston: Houghton Mifflin.

Thoreau, H.D. (1964). Walden. In C. Bode (Ed.), *The portable Thoreau, rev. ed.* (pp. 258-72). New York: Viking Press.

Toch, H., & Smith, H.C. (Eds.). (1968). *Social perception : The development of interpersonal impressions*. Princeton, NJ: D. Van Nostrand.

Turnbull, C.M. (1961). *The forest people: A study of the Pygmies of the Congo*. New York: Clarion.

Vaillant, G.E. (1977). *Adaptation to life*. Boston: Little, Brown and Company.

van Gennep, A. (1960). *Rites of passage* (M. Vizedom & G. Chaffee, Trans.). Chicago: University of Chicago Press.

von Bertalanffy, L. (1967). *Robots, men and minds: Psychology in the modern world*. New York: George Braziller.

Waley, A. (Ed. & Trans.). (1938). *The analects of Confucius*. New York: Random House.

Watts, A.W. (1951). *The wisdom of insecurity: A message for an age of anxiety*. New York: Vintage Books.

Watzlawick, P. (1976). *How real is real? Confusion, disinformation, communication*. New York: Vintage Books.

Watzlawick, P., Weakland, J.H., & Fisch, R. (1974). *Change: Principles of problem formation and problem resolution*. New York: W.W. Norton.

Weathersby, R.P., & Tarule, J.M. (1980). Adult development: Implications for higher education. *AAHE-ERIC/Higher Education Research Report, 4*.

Werner, H. (1948). *Comparative psychology of mental development.* New York: Science Editions.

Wharton, E. (1934). *A backward glance.* New York: D. Appleton-Century.

Wiener, N. (1967). *The human use of human beings: Cybernetics and society.* New York: Avon Books.

Wispe, L.G. (1968). Sympathy and empathy. In D.L. Sills (Ed.), *The international encyclopedia of social science, Vol. 15* (pp. 441-447). New York: The Free Press.

Wlodkowski, R.L. (1985). *Enhancing Adult motivation to learn: A guide to improving instruction and increasing learner achievement.* San Francisco: Jossey-Bass.

INDEX

ABOUT THE AUTHOR

Douglas L. Robertson received his Ph.D. from Syracuse University in 1978. While a Watson Fellow and a Cressey-James Fellow at Syracuse, he lived for a year in Mexico and completed research on Mexican urban life. Since 1977, he has been a teacher, counselor, and program manager at Marylhurst College, a small, liberal arts institution in Portland, Oregon, which is known for its innovative, adult programs. At Marylhurst, he is currently Chair of the Social Science Department and Director of the Human Studies Program. In addition, he teaches adult development and adult learning and advises graduate students in the postsecondary doctoral program at Portland State University. Since 1986, he has been a member of the Northwest Regional Advisory Committee for the Council for Adult and Experiential Learning (CAEL). In 1987, he received a CAEL Northwest Regional Research Grant in order to conduct a feasibility study for joint ventures among industry, labor, and education. He has published numerous academic articles and frequently gives academic presentations, trainings, and consultations on issues related to adult learning, adult development, and international education.